THERE IS NO MAP IN HELL

THE RECORD-BREAKING RUN ACROSS
THE LAKE DISTRICT FELLS

THERE IS NO MAP IN HELL

STEVE BIRKINSHAW

Vertebrate Publishing, Sheffield
www.v-publishing.co.uk

'A wince-inducing insight into what it takes to break epic fell-running records, told with the sort of reluctance and humility that makes Birkinshaw all the more of a hero. I loved the book.'

DAMIAN HALL, OUTDOOR JOURNALIST AND ULTRAMARATHON RUNNER

'He modestly describes the toll it takes as his body gradually disintegrates over the seven days, and also the difficulties the fatigue gives him afterwards. If you like extreme challenges, this is a brilliant unravelling of the preparation and effects of Steve's navigation to and through hell.'

STEVE CHILTON, FELL RUNNER AND AUTHOR OF SEVERAL POPULAR RUNNING BOOKS, INCLUDING *IT'S A HILL, GET OVER IT*

'The world of ultra running has many ordinary people doing extraordinary things, but none more so than Steve Birkinshaw. In this book Steve tells his own remarkable story from his childhood exploits in orienteering to his record-breaking six-day 214-peak Wainwrights run. The aftermath of this huge effort saw Steve suffer with an unknown illness linked with fatigue, and he tells this side of his story with openness and emotion. **There is no Map In Hell** is a story of a family man with a yearning for adventure in the hills, and is a book that any runner will love.'

ANDY NUTTALL, *ULTRA* MAGAZINE

'A very entertaining, revealing and highly readable account of this top mountain runner's trials and tribulations on trail races and record-breaking attempts – most notably the Wainwrights. It's a fascinating insight into what drives Steve to push himself quite so incredibly hard. A must-read this summer!'

CLAIRE MAXTED, *TRAIL RUNNING* MAGAZINE

'The book is a fascinating account of what makes Steve tick and I am seriously impressed with both Steve's determination and the book. The book is a compelling read by a nice but extremely tough person that has pushed his body to the limit of what it can take.'

BILLY BLAND, BOB GRAHAM ROUND RECORD HOLDER AND FORMER CHAMPION FELL RUNNER

'There is no Map in Hell is a frank, personal, yet inspiring account of an ultra-endurance feat few could comprehend. Steve's book is a tour-de-force of the Lake District Wainwrights, detailing a once in a gene-ration record, which was only possible thanks to Steve's lifetime of mountain running experience, and the strength of personality to suck up suffering like few could imagine.'

SHANE OHLY, RACE DIRECTOR – BERGHAUS DRAGON'S BACK RACE

'This is a captivating account of a seriously extreme journey. The tales of preparation and recovery are as fascinating as the meticulous detail of the record-breaking run itself.'

DAVID MCCABE, EDITOR OF *THE FELLRUNNER* MAGAZINE

'I found the book fascinating from start to finish. Steve's writing style is genuine and matter of fact. He doesn't hide any details, from stresses as a child, to his suffering and emotion during the Wainwrights challenge. Nor does he embellish the narrative with unnecessary self-promotion. Instead he tells it like it is, from the heart. This is an awe-inspiring account of an amazing achievement, and an inspiration for what is possible doing something you love. Definitely worth reading!'

DUNCAN ARCHER, ORIENTEER AND MOUNTAIN-MARATHON RUNNER

STEVE BIRKINSHAW

First published in 2017 by Vertebrate Publishing. Reprinted 2017.

Vertebrate Publishing
Crescent House, 228 Psalter Lane, Sheffield S11 8UT.
www.v-publishing.co.uk

This book is a work of non-fiction based on the life, experiences and recollections of Steve Birkinshaw.
In some limited cases the names of people, places, dates and sequences or the detail of events have been
changed solely to protect the privacy of others. The author has stated to the publishers that, except in
such minor respects not affecting the substantial accuracy of the work, the contents of the book are true.

A CIP catalogue record for this book is available from the British Library.

978-1-910240-94-6 (Paperback)
978-1-910240-95-3 (Ebook)

Design and production by Jane Beagley. Cover design by Nathan Ryder.
Vertebrate Publishing
www.v-publishing.co.uk

Vertebrate Publishing is committed to printing on paper from sustainable sources.

Printed and bound in Scotland by Bell & Bain Ltd.

CONTENTS

FOREWORD

BY JOSS NAYLOR MBE

I have lived all my life in the Wasdale valley and being out on the Lake District fells means everything to me. Some of my earliest memories are of being out on the fells, and these memories have stayed with me for my whole life.

When I was about four years old I went out with my brother, Scott, who was nine at the time, to collect sheep on Yewbarrow. I kept asking Scott, 'how much further?', and he would say 'that crag there, that is the top', and when we got over the crag and looked up I thought to myself 'this fell *has no top!*' I also clearly remember going up to Mickledore between Scafell and Scafell Pike when I was about five. There were some hikers going up Broad Stand and they disturbed some ring ouzels nesting on Scafell Crag – it was good to see them, as you see these birds less and less nowadays. From those days as a child I never lost the love of the fells through many years of sheep farming and running on them. This year I turned eighty, and I am still out on the fells. I help my son, Paul, with his sheep on the fells above Wasdale. I also regularly go up the fells near my house, although these days I use sticks to take the pressure off my legs and so protect my badly damaged knee.

In 1986 Andy Ligema and Colin Dulson suggested to me that I might have a go at running round all 214 Wainwright fells. I was worried that it would take too much setting up, but I was lucky enough to have Ken Ledward come on board and help with all the planning. The first two days were roasting hot but went well. On the third day my shoes fell to bits, which was a disaster. However, the biggest disaster was that when I got a new pair of shoes, the webbing was too high and it rubbed up on my ankle bones. It was so bad that I could see the ligament showing. It was a pain that bit into me all day – there was no let-up from it. There was this stinging sensation that never went away, even when I stopped; it was sore like red-hot needles shoved into my ankles. The last two days I could not eat; I was drained to a point I had never been to before. It was as though someone had got hold of me and squeezed all the energy out of me, and then I still had to march for two more days to the finish. When I eventually finished, there was absolutely nothing left in my body.

Looking back now, doing the Wainwrights was a great experience that I would not have liked to miss and I put down a time that was the best I could do. It was one of the hardest things I have ever done, but despite the pain I never got the feeling I wasn't going to finish it. The memories of the hard times and the suffering I experienced during those seven days have faded and now I remember the good times. In particular, the friendships created during that run that have lasted a lifetime. I still find it unbelievable the amount of time people put in on my behalf to support me and I will always be very grateful. It is something special about the sport of fell running that people go out of their way to help one another.

I have known of Steve's running and navigational ability on the fells for many years. He has had many wins at mountain marathons and has won the Lake District Mountain Trial – a special event for me that I have competed in fifty times and won nine times. Steve and I chatted a couple of times before his attempt at completing the Wainwrights. I was very happy to encourage him and to offer advice, such as the importance of taking it one step at a time rather than thinking of the long days and fells ahead, and also advice on nutrition and sitting in a cold beck at the end of every day.

I was delighted when I heard that Steve broke my record; I know the effort and pain that must be gone through to achieve this. Afterwards, it was wonderful to be able to share a stage with him at the Keswick Mountain Festival and for us both to talk about our experiences of the challenge.

It is a pleasure to be able to write this foreword for Steve, particularly as he has used his run of the Wainwrights to raise money for multiple-sclerosis charities, a cause for which I have also raised money in the past. It is important that the effort, planning and toughness of running the Wainwrights is documented, and Steve's is an incredible story of dedication and strength of will, which gives an insight into the seriousness of committing to such a task.

His story will encourage walkers and runners on to the Lake District fells, and to enjoy them as I always have.

Joss.

Joss Naylor
Wasdale, April 2016

PROLOGUE

I'm standing on the steps of the Moot Hall in Keswick. It is a few minutes before nine o'clock in the morning and the market traders are setting up. I have about twenty friends ready to cheer me off on the biggest challenge of my life. For the last year I have been preparing to run round all 214 Wainwright fells in the English Lake District as fast as possible, a massive route of 519 kilometres with 35,000 metres of ascent. With a plan of completing the route in under seven days, I will need to run the equivalent of around two marathons and four times up and down the UK's highest mountain, Ben Nevis, every day. However, I have really been preparing for this moment all my life, from when I started orienteering at age seven until I have reached the point where I feel I can take on this enormous challenge.

After all the preparation I am desperate to set off. Sorting out the route, support, food and logistics has been very intense. However, I'm also scared. Scared of the pain I expect to push myself through over the next seven days. The accounts of the people who have completed the challenge – Alan Heaton and Joss Naylor – as well as showing a love of the fells, are accounts of suffering and of pushing themselves through enormous amounts of pain. I hope I don't suffer like them.

The clock strikes nine and I set off down the steps, a twisting route past all the market stalls, a quick wave at my family and friends and down a little alleyway towards the fells. If all goes to plan, I will return to the Moot Hall in just under seven days, elated at having completed my challenge. However, if it goes wrong and I go through hell will I be strong enough mentally and physically to push through it and carry on?

1 I Have Always Run

Overleaf: Orienteering on the North Yorkshire Moors, 1977 (aged nine). Photo: Steve Birkinshaw Collection.

01   STARTING OUT

'I did it!' Crossing the finish line of the 1976 British Orienteering Championships, I say these words to my mother and then burst into tears. It is just before my eighth birthday and I have completed my course in Cropton Forest, North Yorkshire, in two hours and twenty-four minutes. I am in the M12B class, M12 being for boys younger than twelve and B (as opposed to A) being the less-good class. I come in last by twenty minutes, but the important thing is I have completed the course. This means that my club – the West Anglia Orienteering Club – have won the team competition. Even though we were the *only* team. As well as me, there is my brother, Julian, who finished in the middle, and family friend, Alan Braggins, who finished second to last. An hour later we go up on to the podium to collect our certificates. I am so small I trip trying to get up the step.

I have only vague memories of what I did in the forest to take two hours and twenty-four minutes. My two-kilometre course had ten controls or checkpoints which I had to navigate round in sequence, and which the winner completed in thirty-six minutes. As it was an easy course for young children the controls were just off paths and tracks and I seem to remember I found most of them without too many problems, but one of the controls I just could not seem to find. I would leave the track and go into the forest, but I wasn't leaving the track at the correct point. The frustration of not being able to find the control meant I started to cry. A passing walker saw me crying and tried to help but was not much better than me; I think the orienteering-specific map, rather than the standard UK Ordnance Survey map, confused her. Eventually I followed someone else on the same course into the control. This was usual for my orienteering at this time; I got round by a mixture of asking people, following people and trying (but usually failing) to make sense of the map. There were lots of tears but I was never forced to go orienteering, in fact I was desperate to go out and determined to get round the course, however long it took.

It's funny that determination in an adult is seen as an attribute, whereas similar characteristics in a child are seen as stubbornness and awkwardness. I did have plenty of stubbornness and awkwardness, and it obviously helped me get round orienteering courses, but it also drove my parents, my older siblings, Karen and Julian, and my younger sister, Hilary, mad. I would regularly fly off in a rage or a tantrum. I was known by my siblings as the 'Special Case', 'SC' or 'Swimming Club', as my parents always had to deal with me differently and carefully. The few times my parents argued it was all about how to deal with my rages. On one occasion after a particularly bad rage, my dad, Ian, wanted me to promise that it would never happen again. I refused as I said it was impossible to promise such a thing but that I would do my best, and my mum, Sue, took my side as it seemed like a logical argument.

Part of my frustrations came from the difficulties I had expressing myself. I started off being barely able to talk until I was three years old as I was tongue-tied, a condition where there is a tight piece of skin between the underside of the tongue and the floor of the mouth. This required an operation in hospital and my first ever memory is of being in hospital just before this operation. After this I still struggled really badly with my reading and writing. As a seven year old these were well below average for my age and so different from my excellent mathematical and logic ability that my parents went to see a specialist. They were told I could probably be classed as dyslexic, or they could just let me get on with life, without such a classification, and see how I coped. My parents thought it was best that I just coped with it, so that is what happened. My reading gradually improved, although it is still very slow, but I still have problems writing. I have these thoughts in my head but transferring them from my head to a piece of paper is something I struggle with.

My awkwardness extended to my diet. I refused to eat most foods and ended up living mostly on breakfast cereals, toast and fruit. Unlike many children I refused to have a story at night before I went to sleep. Instead, I wanted to play a game. So every night my mum would play a game with me, but the difficulty was that I would only go to bed when I had won the game. Even harder for my mum was that if I saw that she was deliberately letting me win I would get very cross. So she had to work out clever ways of letting me win without me noticing.

I was very attached to a puppet rabbit called 'Haddit'. It was black and white and fitted on my child's fingers perfectly, with holes for the legs and arms and one for the head. The head was really hard which was important. When my siblings started to annoy me, I would get really cross and say 'you've Haddit', then I would put the rabbit on my hand and try to hit them with it. On one occasion Karen and her friend, Karen Burns, went into the shower cubicle in our house to protect themselves from me and Haddit. They were standing there scared while Haddit was banging and banging on the cubicle door. But no one could ever get cross with me as it wasn't me hitting them but Haddit the rabbit.

Although I was often cross and angry, I was happy and my stresses went when I was out orienteering by myself. There were no people to annoy me, nobody around telling me what to do; it was just me trying to complete the challenge of finishing the course as fast as possible. I would quite often cry, but these were frustrations at my own lack of ability and my determination to get round the course as fast as possible.

The first British orienteering events took place in the 1950s and 1960s, and by the 1970s there were regular events throughout the country. My whole family (apart from Hilary, who preferred team sports) enjoyed orienteering, due to the combination of an individual running sport together with the mental challenge of navigating. So if an event was organised within a two-hour drive of home we would attend – for the big events we went even further afield. Eventually my map-reading skills improved, although I was very unreliable and would still have some disastrous days.

The 1977 British Orienteering Championships were in Cannock Chase, Staffordshire, and I was delighted to come third in the M10 class – a class for children ten and under that had just been introduced. I went up to collect my prize from Denis Howell, minister of sport, and my picture appeared in the *National Orienteering* magazine.

However, I missed the next year's championships as I was recovering from a bad mastoids infection in my ear. For years I had been taking regular courses of antibiotics due to really painful earache. They helped for a bit then the earache would return, keeping me awake at night, and making me even more temperamental. Eventually it blew up into a full infection; for several days I was throwing up anything I tried to eat or drink and the room seemed to spin round and round. I said to my mum 'Will I die?' which was a possibility, especially as her sister had died from a mastoids infection when she was a child. I was rushed to hospital and had an immediate operation to release the pressure in my head and two more operations to sort it out. I spent ten days in hospital and lost a third of my body weight. Afterwards, I was still desperate to go to the championships but my parents wouldn't let me. In fact, I cried more and was more upset about missing it than being ill in the first place. Clearly, not going was the right thing to do as it took me a long time to recover. For six months I could not manage a full school day; I used to arrive a couple of hours late every morning. It was over a year until I could run as fast as I could before my spell in hospital.

As a result of all this I ended up being nearly deaf in one ear. This deafness has made social situations with background noise difficult, and

I think it has made me even quieter in large social groups, as I always have to concentrate really hard to keep up with the conversation and I often miss quite a lot. It also means I have no idea where a sound is coming from, which is hard when someone calls out my name. It can look a bit funny when I have to turn all the way around until I see someone waving or smiling at me. The one advantage of my deafness is that I am better at sleeping in noisy rooms – by putting my good ear to the pillow almost all sound disappears.

My first experience of endurance walking/running was when I was aged eleven. My brother Julian and a friend had decided to do the Chiltern Marathon, a Long Distance Walkers Association (LDWA) marathon-distance walk/run around the Chiltern Hills north-west of London on footpaths and bridleways. I wanted to do it, but my mum said I was too young. After a lot of persuasion she said I could do it if we did it together. So that's what we did. She and I ran the descents and some of the flat sections and walked the rest, working out our average speed and expected finishing time as we progressed, to keep us entertained. Eventually we finished in seven hours and twenty minutes. We had to navigate a bit, and at one point a huge group of people followed us the wrong way across a field. I don't remember it being that hard, just a bit tedious, but my mum suffered with her toenails, which turned black and fell off a few weeks later. It's still the furthest she has ever run or walked in a single day.

In 1981 my dad changed jobs, becoming a director in a chemical company, so we moved from near Cambridge up to Altrincham in south Manchester (my mum gave up her job, which was right at the forefront of computer-software development, just before my sister Karen was born). In many ways the move north was good as we carried on orienteering, and we went up to events in the Lake District National Park in the north-west corner of England. The Lake District is often known as the most beautiful corner of England due to its lakes and mountains, or fells. I enjoyed orienteering in the rough conifer plantations, the beautiful deciduous forests and best of all on the upland fells, with their mix of rough grass-land, heather, boulders and bracken, and of course the amazing views.

At home I also started to do some running training, as I wanted to improve my orienteering. This included training every Wednesday with the local Manchester and District Orienteering Club (MDOC). These training runs started from people's houses over the south Manchester region, and I found running with other people a great way to push myself. As I improved I was selected for the North West Junior Orien-teering Squad, with weekends away in the Lake District. I was part of a great group of orienteering friends: Brendan Bolland, Killian Lomas, Chris O'Donnell, to name a few. We obviously all enjoyed running, navi-gating and racing against each other. We even had training weekends just for our small group, which Brendan organised at his home in Formby, north of Liverpool. Although we were competitive and wanted to beat each other, I don't remember any nasty rivalry between us. It was all very encouraging and in national competitions it was more important that we beat people from other regions rather than each other. I normally ended up behind Killian and Brendan, and this made me determined to do more training and improve.

The fact that the orienteering was going well for me was important, as I didn't fit in at school. When we moved to south Manchester I changed schools to Altrincham Grammar School for Boys, the local selective state school for the top fifty per cent of boys who passed an entrance exam. Moving into a new school in the middle of year 8, or year 2 as it was called back then, was always going to be difficult. This was especially true for me as I immediately stood out as different. I had a posh Cambridge accent, I was exceptionally quiet and shy, I had greasy hair in a bowl cut and I was also one of the smallest in my class. In each year the classes were streamed for academic ability and I was put in the second highest of five classes. Unfortunately it was probably the wrong class, as at the end-of-year exams, after I had been there for just a term, I finished top overall. I was well ahead of everyone in maths, science subjects, geography and even history (I have a good short-term memory) and about average in English. People started to make fun of me.

Unfortunately it got worse the next year. I remember in particular one incident in music class. We were all sitting on the desks so we could see. One of the other boys in the class decided to annoy me by deliberately sitting in front of me so I couldn't see. I should have pushed him away but I didn't want to make a fuss, so I sat behind him, gradually becoming more and more bored. The pocket of the jacket he was wearing was coming apart a bit and had a loose thread, so I sat there playing with the thread. After the class had finished some of the other boys said I was feeling his bottom and that I was gay. It was obviously not true and I'm not sure if they actually believed it, but it was another excuse to pick on me. For a while this made me sad; it was hard being in a class without any real friends and with some people making fun of me. But I thought about it quite a lot and I realised that in a group of children there is often someone picked on or teased. Unfortunately it was me. But I knew that as well as being different I was partly being picked on because they were jealous of my academic ability. I decided I could not change, I would just be myself and that I was tough enough mentally to take it. I knew in the long term I would probably end up with a happy life, which some of those being nasty to me would never achieve. So when I went to school I would speak very little, ignore any nasty comments and just get on with doing the work. Luckily I had the weekend and orienteering for my freedom and happiness.

Despite being small for my age I was still achieving good results against my peers in orienteering races. The biggest UK orienteering event of the year, the JK, takes place every Easter and in 1984 took place in North Wales. The course for that year was on rough open fell with lots of climbing, and this suited me. I finished fourth alongside the top orienteers in the country of my age group. Soon after the JK, Killian and Brendan – despite finishing behind me – were selected for a British junior team development tour to Ludvika in Sweden. I wasn't selected, and was extremely disappointed. So I wrote a letter to the chairman of the selectors explaining why I thought I should go. They were really surprised to receive a letter from a child rather than a parent, and my determination and commitment obviously made a good impression. Soon after I also had a reasonable run at that year's British Orienteering Championships, and so I was given a last-minute place on the tour. I was delighted and enjoyed the first of many great orienteering tours to Scandinavia. Although on pure speed I was slower than most of my contemporaries, I seemed to be able to train harder and go for longer over rougher terrain than almost anyone else. It was gradually dawning on me that I was suited to the longer competitions with rough forests, rocks and hills – the tougher the better.

Karen and Julian started to do the Karrimor International Mountain Marathon (KIMM) when they were eighteen. This event takes place annually at the end of October and involves two long days of mountain navigation, running with a rucksack containing everything needed for the hills and an overnight camp. In those days this was the only event of its kind, whereas nowadays there are lots of similar mountain marathon events (it's now called the Original Mountain Marathon, or OMM). With up to 2,000 pairs taking part it was a prestigious event to win, and the elite class is still the blue ribbon event for mountain marathons in the UK. I was desperate to join my siblings in competing but the minimum age was sixteen with one of the pair needing to be eighteen. So as soon as I turned sixteen I asked my dad to run with me. Luckily he agreed, as that year it was nearby in the Peak District between Manchester and Sheffield. We entered the 'score' class, where the aim was to get as many checkpoints as possible in six hours on the first day and five hours on the second day. Over the two days we reached fifteen checkpoints and scored 340 points, and that put us in the top twenty per cent in the score class. We both carried heavy rucksacks and had a lot of very unsuitable clothing. I ran in tracksuit bottoms, which got really heavy when wet, and I remember spending much of the weekend pulling them up. I had a great time, but my dad hated it (especially the camping) and never did anything similar again. I took part in each of the next three years' events, with a second place in the B class with my brother and a third in the A class with an orienteering friend from university, Neil Conway. Although they were hard work, on each occasion I was the stronger member of the team and I always enjoyed the whole weekend. The wind, rain and navigation added to the fun and made the weekends really memorable. When I ran with my brother it was in the Galloway Hills in Scotland and it rained heavily for much of the race. My main memory of the weekend was coming to a slow-moving but very deep river just before it flowed into a lake. Many of the teams were just standing about wondering what to do. We gained lots of time as we just jumped in and swam across without any hesitation.

One thing really affected my running during this period of my life, both my enjoyment of running and my performances. This was that sometimes I would get really sore bowels while running, which could be agony when I finished and for several hours afterwards. After one orienteering event, the pain was so bad I went to hospital with suspected appendicitis. The problem was that as I ran I would get a build-up in pressure at a particular point in my bowel. This would get more painful until I could do a big fart, and then there would be relief for a couple of minutes before the cycle started again, but with more pain than the previous time. Visits to the doctors didn't help, as it was a problem that occurred only while running and only sporadically, so was not high on their list of priorities. However, I thought I could work out what the problem was. I needed to if I was going to compete and enjoy running at a high level. With this determination I wrote a diary of what I ate and when over an entire year. Gradually it became obvious that, as well as an egg intolerance, the time at which I was eating was also really important. The problem normally occurred when I ran in the evening, and earlier in the day it only occurred if I ran more than four hours after breakfast. So it seemed that with the food at a particular place in my bowels, the shaking around and the diverting of the blood supply to my muscles was causing the problem. Ever since, I have avoided any big meals between four and twelve hours before a long or fast run. This generally seems to have worked, which is an amazing relief. The problem also seems to have got slightly better as I have got older, which I think is because I'm generally not eating as much.

By my final year as a junior orienteer I had moved to Nottingham university to study for a mathematics degree. I was one of the top-four junior orienteers in the UK. We had a great group of us: Neil Conway (who was also at Nottingham), Simon Bourne, Richard Baxter and Steve Nicholson (who were at Cambridge university). The best thing was our monthly trip up to the Lake District to stay at Ambleside youth hostel for training weekends. We really enjoyed running through the forests and fells, training hard and just messing around. Despite injury problems with one of my calf muscles, I managed a third place at the British Orienteering Championships and a thirty-second place at the World Junior Orienteering Championships in Belgium.

Around this time I also did my first Lake District fell race and my first week of fell running in the Lake District. My regular group of orienteering friends and I were spending New Year in a camping barn at Derwent Hill outdoor centre (thanks to Richard's dad) near Keswick. We did the Wansfell Race up and down from Ambleside. It was great fun: sixteen minutes of pain climbing up to the top of the fell, and then six minutes descending at full speed where one misplaced step would result in a very nasty fall. With my background of many years' orienteering through rough forests and fells, I found I was good on the descent and overtook quite a lot of people. Although, as I was used to only short bursts rather than a 300-metre descent, my quadriceps were agony for the next few days – the first time I had suffered from the classic DOMS (Delayed Onset Muscle Soreness). Later in the week I also tried to jump over a fence, but failed. My foot got stuck between the top two wires, leaving me dangling from the fence with some nasty ligament damage. Despite this I still enjoyed a long run on the fells every day. Over the week there was also a lot of drinking, and I managed to get thrown out of the night-club in Keswick for some mad dancing and was nearly arrested for trying to roll up the white lines in the middle of the road ...

At university I became a vegetarian. As well as being fussy about food I also never liked eating meat or fish. I didn't like the taste of it, or the thought of eating dead animals. But for many years I was persuaded to eat meat by my parents as I was told it was good for me. Then I read a study in a newspaper that said vegetarians live longer than people who eat meat, so the argument about meat being good for you seemed to be false. However, it felt like a major step to become a complete vegetarian. The final straw was when I was back at home in the Easter holidays after two terms at university. For our meal one evening my mum prepared some spare ribs. The fact that the meat was so obviously taken straight from an animal meant that while I was eating it I could not get the thought of this dead pig out of my head. I didn't say anything at the time, but when I returned to university at the end of the Easter holidays I changed to the vegetarian meal options at the hall of residence and told my family when I returned home at the end of that term that I was a vegetarian. I haven't deliberately eaten meat or fish since then (apart from a piece of snake meat!) and I have never felt like I wanted to. Being a vegetarian has certainly made me think carefully about food, so I always look at the ingredients and the nutritional content of everything I buy, which is obviously no bad thing. Whether I run faster because of a meat-free diet I don't know, but it doesn't seem to have done me any harm and it feels the right decision for me.

02   RUNNING TAKES OVER

When I started at university I joined the Nottingham University Orienteering Club. There were a number of freshers who joined the club at the same time, and one was Emma Moody. Emma had done bits of orienteering before and was encouraged to join the club by her best friend for many years, Sue Loughlin. Sue was also a friend of mine from the North West Junior Orienteering Squad. Emma and I really enjoyed being in the club, both going to orienteering events and the socials, and we got on very well. However, in the first year at university we were both in relationships with other people. By the start of our second year we were both single and started to see a lot more of each other, including many hours talking long into the night at parties. I thought that Emma was intelligent, beautiful, loving and kind and I also loved her inner toughness and determination. Eventually I plucked up the courage to ask her out and we have been together ever since. We've now been married for twenty happy years.

Unfortunately, soon after we began our relationship I got badly injured. Where the tendon joins the bottom of the kneecap it became very inflamed in both knees. To say I was really bad at coping with not being able to run is an understatement. Emma was great at putting up with me when I got fed up of not being able to go out. My fix of running to remove the stresses and strains of my life was not possible. Swimming was just about OK on my knee, but ploughing up and down a busy swimming pool was a very poor alternative to the freedom of running. Eventually, after about twelve months, I was back to running short distances, but was still pretty worried about trying anything longer. In fact, my knees and legs hurt quite badly when I started running. After another eighteen months on a world trip – including a lot of walking and fruit picking – my knees seemed fully recovered and I could start running properly again.

After our world trip I wondered what sort of job to apply for. In the end I decided to continue my education and I pursued an MSc in hydrology at Newcastle University. I had some interest in hydrology and was keen to be based near the Lake District where Emma was working and had family. It was, of course, somewhere we also loved to run. However, I had clearly not been thinking for long about doing hydrology, as while orienteering at night during that year I fell over and banged my head on a tree. I concussed myself and was found wandering randomly around the forest in my running kit – which is obviously quite dangerous on a cold winter's night. When I eventually got back to the warmth of a car I was asked what I was studying and I thought I was back at Nottingham doing a mathematics degree. When told I was actually studying an MSc in hydrology I replied 'Why the hell am I doing that?' The worst thing for my housemates and fellow orienteers in Newcastle who were looking after me – Jake Gilmore and Jo Durham – was that I had chipped a tooth, and every time I felt it with my tongue I told them what I had done but without remembering I had previously said it. After the thirtieth time Jake and Jo were both running out of patience.

Eventually they took me to hospital where I spent the night. I woke up the next morning back to my normal self but very confused as to why I was in hospital; I had no memory of what had happened. To start with I thought I had gone on a mad drinking session, but that didn't really make sense as I didn't have a hangover or smell of alcohol. Eventually Jake and Jo turned up and explained all. I was a bit annoyed about being told that I had to go home and rest rather than go orienteering.

Emma and I married in May 1995. A month before this we had the British Universities Orienteering Championships weekend. At the social on the Saturday night we got the chance to try sumo wrestling wearing huge padded suits. Unfortunately on my bout I rolled over the top of the guy I was wrestling, and fell badly on the big toe of my left foot. After two days of throbbing I got it X-rayed and there was a small chip of bone at the joint just near the ball of my foot. After only a week's rest I started running (the JK orienteering event was taking place and I was desperate not to miss it) and ever since then the joint has been swollen and I scream in agony if I accidently kick a rock with that toe. By the morning of our wedding I was finally giving it a chance to heal so went cycling instead of running. I descended round a tight corner on a narrow road only to see a car coming the other way. I braked but the only way to avoid the car was to cycle off the road. I ended up on my back in amongst some nettles. Luckily there was no serious damage but I did spend the rest of our wedding day desperately trying to avoid rubbing my sore and itchy back.

After my MSc I continued with a PhD at Newcastle. Both Emma and I trained hard to improve our orienteering so we could get into the British team for the world championships. Neither of us quite made it, making the British orienteering squad but just missing out on the team. However, we also started to do the longer fell races and mountain marathons together. Emma seemed to be naturally good at the long-distance fell races; over a couple of years she was first lady in nearly all the Lake District classic long-distance fell races. She always finished with a big smile on her face whereas I would run in with a massive grimace and then collapse in a heap after getting over the finishing line. As a mixed team we also won the elite class at several mountain marathons.

Unfortunately Emma started to get injury problems soon after this. A slightly sticking-out heel bone rubbed on the hard heel cup of her running shoes and the bone gradually grew and started to interfere with her Achilles tendon. First running became painful, and then agony, and finally even walking any distance became really painful. Eventually both feet needed operating on (separately, six months apart) and the big lumps of extra bone on her heels were removed. Recovery has been good and she can do long fell walks and some short runs, but her heels still get sore after a long run. Since the injury and the operation she has been brilliant to me and focused her energies on letting me achieve my goals, and more recently also looking after our children when I am out on the fells.

After finishing my PhD I started a post-doctoral research post at Newcastle University while Emma was working in Carlisle, and so we lived in the Tyne Valley between Carlisle and Newcastle. First we lived at Haltwhistle and then at Haydon Bridge. As Emma was injured I was looking for a new mountain marathon partner for the KIMM. I was lucky enough to be asked by Mark Seddon – who would go on to win the KIMM/OMM elite class ten times – to run the 1997 KIMM with him. It was great to run with Mark and learn from his expertise. His attention to detail was extremely impressive. I had always tried to carry a light pack with me in mountain marathons but he had taken it to another level. He checked which batteries I had in my head torch as different ones have different weights. We also slept on bubble wrap and threw it away on the morning of the second day, which is allowed at the KIMM/OMM but not at many other mountain marathons. Another trick I stole from him is clipping a mug on to my waist belt so it is quick and easy to grab and drink water as I cross a stream. I was delighted to win the mountain marathon with Mark and we also won together in 1998 and 1999.

Since then I have won the elite class in numerous other mountain marathons (over twenty in total) including four others at the KIMM/OMM (to make seven in total). I have also completed the elite class at the KIMM/OMM nineteen times. The one I was happiest with I ran with Morgan Donnelly, a running friend who lived close by in the Tyne valley and who was British Fell Running Champion in 2011, in the Cheviot Hills in 2002. Running with Mark I always felt I was in his shadow.

However, it was completely different with Morgan; although Morgan is a great runner his navigation is not good enough to do well in a mountain marathon, so it was up to me to get the navigation correct and I did.

Around this time I took up a new sport: adventure racing. This combination of off-road running or trekking, mountain biking, and kayaking or canoeing, all with a navigational element was just beginning to take off in the UK with 'ACE Races'. I competed individually in these races and due to my running and navigational ability I regularly won them, including winning the ACE Race series of four races one year. For this I received as a prize a 4x4 car for a year. At mountain biking I was extremely bad at descending but OK climbing, and especially good at carrying my bike over the rough sections. My technique and ability at kayaking and canoeing was awful (particularly as I am missing one of the pectoral muscles on my right side) but my determination meant I didn't lose too much time.

As well as winning individual races I was also part of several successful teams that won lots of UK races and the British championships on several occasions. As part of a team I also competed in international races throughout the world, coming seventh at the 2001 World Championship in Switzerland and getting a top-three position in several other races. The 2001 World Championship was a multi-day continuous race. I was in a team with the Davies family: Jim, Andrew and Nic. They lived nearby in Cumbria, and although mostly fell runners they had also started adventure racing and seemed to excel in any sports they tried. Nic suffered from amazingly bad blisters from the first day onwards. All the skin on the base of her feet seemed to have come off by the time we had finished after five days. It was very impressive to see how much she was suffering while having the mental strength to carry on. It showed me a level of determination I had never seen before, but which I would need to emulate in my Wainwrights run. The whole race also showed me how you can cope with the lack of sleep, as we had fewer than ten hours in those five days. The human body just seems to adapt to going all the time;

you can feel awful and shattered but carry on moving. However, I did realise how bad my decision making and navigation can become as I get tired; I made a four-hour mistake on a mountain-biking section towards the end of the race by taking us up a massive climb on the wrong road.

In October 2003 our first child, James, was born. I realised that I was no longer going to have the time to commit to adventure racing at a top level. If I was going to be involved in looking after James then training for at least three different sports and regular races throughout the UK and abroad was going to be impossible. It's hard to have to give up on a sport you enjoy but I always enjoyed the running side most and I hoped I would have the time to carry on with my running training and enter some races, as long as they weren't too far from where we lived.

But before I settled down to pure running challenges, there was one last big challenge that I took part in. It started four weeks after James was born and it is one of the silliest I have done. All the running and athletic pursuits I take part in I really enjoy, but I did not enjoy quite a lot of this one, and most of the time I spent thinking that I should be at home helping Emma look after James. Four months earlier I went to the Brecon Beacons in Wales to take part in a trial for the BBC2 reality television series *SAS: Are You Tough Enough?* The trial involved going up and down the highest point (Pen y Fan) twice, carrying a rucksack weighing twenty kilograms. Apart from having to do it in walking boots (I do not know why. But in the army you do what you are told …), it was very similar to a lot of my training and I ended up being the fastest. I was selected as one of twenty-four volunteers to go to Namibia and take part in the programme. I thought long and hard about whether to go or not for a couple of reasons. Firstly, as James had been born so recently and, secondly, the idea of being shouted at and ordered around by SAS guys did not really appeal. However, I eventually decided to go as it was too good an opportunity to miss. Basically, it was a free holiday in a beautiful country and a chance to see what military training is like and how

I could cope. If I was not happy I could drop out at any point and go straight home. I also liked the fact that there was no prize for winning, so all the volunteers were going along not for any monetary gain but just to have a go and see what it was like.

We all flew out to Windhoek, the Namibian capital, a couple of days before the sixteen-day course was due to start. This gave us a chance to get to know each other and acclimatise to the severe heat. We were then driven to the huge sand dunes at the coast and the start of the course. The physical and verbal abuse started immediately, and it was made worse for me by the fact that I had eaten some dodgy food in the hotel and was throwing up and had diarrhoea. On the second day, me and another guy were picked out for a 'beasting' session. I'm not sure why we were picked out, but it may have been because we were looking weak and they were hoping we might drop out while being filmed. For an hour we had to run up and down a sand dune, sometimes carrying each other, and doing press-ups at the end of each climb and descent. The heat together with the fact that I was feeling really unwell made it horrendous and, despite not dropping out, it made good TV!

We were supplied with army rations, a lot of which I did not eat, partly as I was ill and also as it contained meat. However, I did swallow a piece of snake meat as it was part of an exercise so it was easier not to refuse it. Once I had recovered from the diarrhoea I was easily the fastest on a twenty-hour solo endurance walk with a heavy rucksack. It was really nice being by myself for a while away from the shouting and aggressive attitude of the military guys. Although I will always remember how hard it was climbing the steep, soft side of a 200-metre-high sand dune, crawling up for nearly an hour only slightly faster than I was sliding back down.

I quit soon afterwards, just as a twelve-hour interrogation was due to start. This was going to involve sitting or standing in various very painful stress positions for long periods of time with an occasional visit to the interrogator to be asked loads of questions in a very aggressive way.

It started to feel very real, rather than just a reality television show, and I felt I should have been at home with my family rather than go through the interrogation. It is funny that if I am in control I can push myself to the limit and cope with a huge amount of pain for long periods of time, but once it's someone else in charge telling me what to do, I cannot cope. The people who seemed to be able to cope on the course were those involved in team sports that were used to being told what to do by coaches. I compete mainly in individual sports where self-motivation is the key.

My dad did not often talk about work at home but I know his colleagues and the people who worked for him respected him. This was because he would always remain calm and listen. When he retired he continued to work as hard as ever, helping small businesses grow. As with many people of his generation he seemed to be really practical – when something went wrong he would just take it apart and mend it (I am the complete opposite and incapable of mending anything). When the family moved to Altrincham he used these skills when he took over the printing of orienteering maps using an offset lithography printer. Each of the five different colours in the maps needed to be printed separately, and the printing needed to be consistent over every sheet of paper and perfectly aligned. My dad was meticulous and spent many, many hours making sure each map was perfect. Not surprisingly he found it quite stressful, especially after a hard day's work. I could see that by the time he reached the fifth colour he would be desperate for it not to go wrong, as if it did he would have to throw thousands of nearly completed maps away.

My mum has also spent and still does spend many hours playing key roles in the organisation of major orienteering events. It's this sort of volunteer work that is vital for keeping many minority sports in the UK (such as orienteering and fell running) going. As my dad got older his results gradually improved against those in his age group. So when he was in the M65 class (sixty-five to seventy-year-old men) he became

British champion. He was looking forward to turning seventy and winning again. But a couple of months before he turned seventy and three months after James was born, he and my mum were on a cruise in the Caribbean when he suddenly found eating impossible. Soon after their return he was diagnosed with oesophageal cancer with a secondary cancer in his liver. He deteriorated very quickly after this and it was very hard seeing him, especially as up until this point he had been so physically active. He died just after his seventieth birthday. As many people find, it made me think a lot about my own life, that of my family, and the importance of enjoying it and making the most of it. Certainly I now appreciate every day with my family more, and also every time I am out running, not knowing how long it will continue for. I also try to follow my dad's example by trying to remain calm, whatever pressure I am under. My dad's death also taught me to look at the big picture. I finally realised that worrying about small things like making a phone call or standing up and talking in front of a group of people is unnecessary. I decided that in these circumstances I needed to just try to be myself and, instead of worrying, to enjoy it.

In 2006 Matthew was born and, in 2008, Hannah. Just before Hannah was born we moved to the Lake District about three kilometres east of the village of Threlkeld and ten kilometres east of Keswick. My mum was struggling to look after the house the family had owned for sixteen years and so we jumped at the chance to move in. It is an isolated old farmhouse in a stunning location, 300 metres along a track from the end of a small road, yet only about a kilometre and a half from the A66 road. The main problem with the house is that we regularly seem to be unable to drive out from it, due to either flooding in the valley which we need to cross, or snow and ice on the steep approach road, but it is worth it to live in such a beautiful location. The timing of moving to the Lake District was great as James was just about to start school and my bosses at Newcastle University were happy for me to work mostly at home, as long as I went to meet them once a week in Newcastle. They knew they could trust me to get the work done wherever I was based. I still do the same work – carrying out research in hydrology. Mainly I am involved in the running and development of computer models, taking rainfall as an input to the model and simulating how the water flows through the ground and into rivers. My children just think I sit at home playing on the computer. Often it is quite like that, but when I have a tight deadline or the model is not working correctly it can get quite stressful. I also have to write reports and articles for academic journals, which I never enjoy.

On moving to the Lake District, I also changed fell-running clubs, moving from Northumberland Fell Runners to Borrowdale Fell Runners. Borrowdale Fell Runners is one of the top fell-running clubs in the country and has members all around the northern Lake District. It was an obvious choice as I was already friends with a lot of the members, like Morgan Donnelly and the Davies family. We are basically a group of individuals who enjoy running and racing hard in the fells. We usually all just go out and train by ourselves but over the winter a group of us meet up every week for a club run up on the fells in the dark. For the first five minutes these are quite sociable, but somewhere along the first climb someone will up the pace and within a few minutes we are all climbing as fast as possible not wanting to get left behind or show any weakness. Often it is a case of 'last man standing', with the pace gradually increasing and people dropping out until only one person is left. After about seventy minutes we will be back at the cars exhausted but happy. These training runs and the proximity of so many great fell races have certainly helped me to get fit. In fact, the only problem I have is to make sure I'm not doing too many fell races; it's easy to do two a week during the spring and summer and start to suffer due to over-racing.

During this period of my life the importance of being in and running over the fells of the Lake District grew. I love running anywhere, but for me the pleasure of running and racing in the Lake District cannot be beaten. It is the freedom to run anywhere I want in the fells without any restrictions that makes me really happy. I started racing more and running further, and began competing in the long distance, classic Lake District fell races, such as the Wasdale (thirty-four kilometres, 2,700 metres of ascent) and Ennerdale fell races (thirty-seven kilometres, 2,300 metres of ascent). The first time I competed in these they were very painful and hard – all I really cared about was finishing, but the more hours I put into training the more enjoyable the long races became. I started racing hard and my times improved. But I wanted to push it further and do longer challenges – and do them well.

03   THE BOB GRAHAM ROUND

The Bob Graham Round is a route of forty-two Lake District peaks that must be completed within twenty-four hours. A successful completion of the round was first achieved by Bob Graham, a hotelier from Keswick, in 1932. The round starts and finishes at the Moot Hall in Keswick and the route is now generally accepted to be around 106 kilometres (66 miles) long with 8,200 metres of ascent. The exact distance depends on how you measure it, whether you use a paper map, mapping software on a computer, or a GPS track of the route. The first person to complete the round after Bob Graham was Alan Heaton in 1960. Since then it has become the ultimate test of fell-running ability with 1,976 completions of the round by the end of 2015 and a men's record of thirteen hours and fifty-three minutes by Billy Bland and a women's record of fifteen hours and twenty-four minutes by Jasmin Paris.

A key feature of the Bob Graham Round – and other similar challenges – is that although a single person is attempting to complete the route, there is usually a big team of people helping them achieve their goal. At any one time there are usually several people – called 'supporters' or 'pacers' – running with the contender. The supporters will do a single section of around four hours before a new team takes over, usually at a road crossing. This support team will be carrying food, drink and spare clothes for the contestant and in some cases will show them the way, especially towards the end as they get really tired. There will also be a road-support team to make sure everyone is well looked after, with warm food and drink at the end of each section. They will also sort out everything the hill-support team need to carry with them and their logistics, such as getting them to the start of a section and back from the finish of a section. The fact that everyone is working together as a team towards a common goal is completely different from a normal fell race, where it is a battle to beat the people you are racing against. I really enjoy both sides of it, but in many ways working together as a team is the best. Being a good supporter is a crucial but difficult job. You need to make sure the contender does not get lost, work out how much and what kinds of food and drink to offer them, and also what sort of moral support they need. Some contenders just need the supporters around with no talking, others want to chat all the way round. Some contenders need continual encouragement while others need to be told to try harder and get going. I try and help other people complete a Bob Graham Round as often as I can, which is usually around three or four times a year.

I first attempted the Bob Graham Round in 1996. I was not very experienced at ultrarunning but hoped I would be good enough to complete it with a small number of supporters. I attempted a clockwise round and started strongly over the first two sections. But on the third section after Dunmail Raise I started to have bowel problems, so I walked most of the section to Scafell Pike. By then my knee was hurting and I gave up at Mickledore after about thirteen hours. Emma and her dad waited for me for four hours with ropes on the rocks of Broad Stand (the climb up to Scafell just after Mickledore, which is the only section on the entire route requiring climbing skills), which I felt really bad about. My knee was sore, though nowadays I would have just carried on as I know it normally gets a bit sore on a long run but it doesn't seem to do any long-term damage. However, in 1996 I was still worried about causing myself a long-term injury, it not having been that long since I had been badly injured previously, so I didn't want to risk it. In those days I also never took any painkillers while running, whereas these days I find they can sometimes make a big difference. I was obviously disappointed not to have completed the entire route, and I shed a few tears at Mickledore, but after a few days I had thought about it a bit more and decided that I was still young and this attempt was a great learning experience. I would come back fitter, stronger and better prepared.

After focusing on running after James's birth, I decided in 2005 to make another Bob Graham Round attempt. This time I was going to be extremely well prepared, so I went out and ran over all the sections of the route several times, making sure I knew the fastest lines. Over a bank holiday weekend about a month before my attempt I also ran the whole route in two long days. On the Saturday I ran from Threlkeld to Wasdale Head via Keswick, rested on Sunday and on the Monday I ran from Wasdale Head back to Threlkeld via Dunmail Raise. It took sixteen hours of running and so I thought that eighteen hours sounded like a sensible schedule. I decided on doing an anti-clockwise attempt, which is unusual as these days over ninety per cent of people do clockwise attempts. This was because I wanted to get the road section over with first and the really rocky section from Great Gable to Rossett Pike completed in the first half.

I set off at the same time as Morgan Donnelly and we had Jon Bardgett (a local mountain biker who had organised some of our adventure racing teams) as our road support and also a good team to support us on the fells with enough people that we could split up if necessary. The day went really well. It was a bit wet to start with and at the end, but most of the day was good for running. I got ahead of Morgan early on in the mist descending Great Gable, but he was gradually closing in on me for the rest of the day. I struggled on the climbs towards the end but descended strongly all day. In the end I finished in seventeen hours and nine minutes, to give me the fifth-fastest time (eighth fastest now), with Morgan finishing fifteen minutes later. I was really happy. I had not only completed the ultimate fell-running challenge, but to do the fifth-fastest time was a major achievement. But I thought I could do better. I wanted to do more long, hard ultraruns.

Interestingly, it took a lot more out of me than I originally realised. A week afterwards I felt OK and started racing again. But a few weeks after that my legs became agony going downhill and I had to drop out of some races and eventually have around four weeks' complete rest before I felt properly recovered. So nowadays, after a twenty-four-hour (or similar length) ultrarun, I always try to have two very easy weeks with just a thirty-minute recovery jog every two or three days. I have also seen other people run very soon after completing a Bob Graham Round but then start to struggle badly, so I recommend a similar very easy couple of weeks for anyone doing such a long and hard ultrarun.

04 THE RAMSAY ROUND AND THE PADDY BUCKLEY ROUND

As well as the Bob Graham Round, there are two other famous twenty-four-hour rounds over British mountains: the Ramsay Round and the Paddy Buckley Round. At the end of 2015, there had been eighty-four completions of the Ramsay Round, and 135 completions of the Paddy Buckley Round.

The Ramsay Round is in Scotland, with a start and finish in Glen Nevis near Fort William. A clockwise round starts up Ben Nevis, then on to the Aonachs, the Grey Corries, then Stob Coire Easain and its twin; it then takes in three Munros (Scottish mountains over 3,000 feet) to the east of Loch Treig before a complete traverse of the Mamores. Like the Bob Graham Round the distance depends on the exact route and how it is measured, but it is generally accepted to be slightly shorter than the Bob Graham at about ninety-three kilometres (fifty-eight miles) with 8,500 metres of ascent. Despite being the shortest of the three rounds it has the smallest number of completions due to the nature of the terrain. The hills are either rocky or rough (heather and tussocks) underfoot; there is very little short, runnable grass. Also, the route doesn't cross any roads (although it does cross a railway). Normally support is received at only two points (compared to four on the Bob Graham Round): at Loch Treig dam (one kilometre from a road) and at Loch Eilde Mor (six kilometres from a road). The round is also in a sparsely populated region and so it is hard to get a good support team. The final aspect that makes it harder than the Bob Graham Round is that the mountains are higher and more exposed than the Lake District, so the weather is often worse.

I thought the Ramsay Round looked like a great route, especially with its wild location and tough terrain. I had also never previously been over forty per cent of the route and the rest of it I had been over only once, which made it even more exciting, although harder to get a fast time. I wondered what the best way to go about doing the round was, due to the difficulties of getting support. But, I thought of a good plan. I booked a cottage in Glen Nevis for a week in June 2006 for my family and my parents-in-law, Joe and Mary. This was just a five-minute walk from the start and finish of the round. When a nice day was forecast I could do a clockwise round starting at 3 a.m. and hopefully finishing soon after 9 p.m., getting close to the then-record of eighteen hours and twenty-three minutes and doing it all in daylight. (The current record is held by Jasmin Paris with a time of sixteen hours and thirteen minutes.) I would run it all by myself, but I could recruit my family and Joe and Mary to walk into the two possible support points to provide me with food and drink. The only thing I could not plan ahead was the weather; bad weather was forecast all week. What should I do? However, on the third day of the holiday the detailed forecast showed there was one possibil-ity: a twenty-hour weather window, if I could set off at 11 a.m. that morn-ing. Even though it was raining, there wasn't much wind and the weather was likely to improve. Hopefully I would be off the hills before the worst of the predicted low-pressure system arrived the next day. But it would entail running through the night over the Mamores. I decided to go for it.

I took the short walk from the cottage to the youth hostel. Emma, Joe, Mary, James and Matthew were there and James said 'Ready, steady, go' and I was off up Ben Nevis. The seven hours over Ben Nevis, the Aonachs, the Grey Corries and Stob Coire Easain went well. The rain came and went, so the rocks were really slippery, and I was in hill fog most of the time. I avoided one of the subsidiary tops on the Grey Corries by going through a corrie and was delighted to get a really good view of a mother and six baby ptarmigans. I was running strongly and I found some decent routes (considering I didn't know the area very well and visibility was so poor) and I even found enough sources of water as there had been so much rain. I met Emma, Joe and James at the midge-infested Loch Treig dam and did a quick transition. The next section of the three eastern hills was hard work but I was still moving OK. Stupidly I forgot to take a bottle or mug with me on this leg (I blame the midges), so I didn't drink enough. I started to struggle on the long track run to the base of the Mamores and I met Joe and Mary at Loch Eilde Mor in a poor way. Within two minutes I was shivering and everything was taking too long in the dark. I found it hard to eat anything but I knew I had to. I was also very nervous about the next section; the first three hours would be in the dark over the rockiest section of the Mamores. As I was so worried I filled my rucksack with a lot of kit and food together with a big head torch before setting off, still shivering, thirty-three minutes after arriving.

During the next couple of hours I got worse physically and then struggled mentally with the whole thing. I became really negative. I started to think what would happen if I tripped and injured myself and how long I would last before I died of hypothermia. Why was I risking my life and the happiness of my family being up on a mountain at night in a bad physical way for some small personal satisfaction? It's hard to get out of this downward spiral of feeling negative and so moving slower, and this in turn perpetuating more negativity. For an hour this negative spiral gripped me and I was ready to get down off the ridge, into Glen Nevis and back to the cottage. However, I eventually managed to turn it around. I rationalised that actually I was safe – I had plenty of good kit with me to survive and the weather was OK. I also realised that running is what I do and what makes me happy and so my family happy. I also started looking at the time and the number of hills left and thought that all I had to do was one summit an hour and I would complete the round in twenty-four hours, which was my main aim.

I ate very little on the Mamore ridge and only had one bottle of water but I was doing better than one summit an hour and gradually realised that I would easily complete the round. Dawn is always a magical time when you have been out running all night. So as it grew lighter my pace increased, although the forecast wind also picked up. I eventually reached the final top, Mullach nan Coirean. I ran really fast down from it and along the road to the finish. I had completed the round in twenty-one hours and two minutes. Appropriately, as I had run the entire round by myself, there was no one at the finish. I walked slowly back to the cottage, briefly said hello to the family and went to sleep happy with my success-ful completion.

Looking back at my report of the round it was obvious I had enjoyed a long and tiring day in the hills. I did really well to complete the route in just over twenty-one hours considering I ran the whole route by myself, the weather conditions were less than ideal, and I lacked a detailed know-ledge of the route. But I was not happy with how long I took at the two transitions. This is currently the eighth-fastest time for the round and the fastest solo round.

Having completed the Ramsay Round I was keen to complete the Paddy Buckley Round so that I had completed all three major rounds. In fact I knew I would not be happy until I had completed the Paddy Buckley Round. I didn't have any important races at the end of August so I thought it was a possibility to do it then. Hopefully I would have the endurance left from the Ramsay Round training; I certainly didn't have the speed to do anything else well. At twenty-seven kilometres long and with 2,000 metres of ascent, the Borrowdale Fell Race at the start of August would be a good test to see if I had recovered sufficiently from the Ramsay Round, and if that felt good I would have a go at the Paddy Buck-ley Round. I felt awful at Borrowdale; I gave up and was ill for the next couple of days. But I decided to do the Paddy Buckley Round anyway.

Fell-running and adventure-racing friends, Tim and Jayne Lloyd, offered their house near Llanberis as a base. Tim would act as road support and he would find some local runners to help. I didn't really know any of the route and having local runners to help was a great bonus. The next thing that needed sorting was to work out what sort of schedule to set. From my previous rounds I reckoned with the support I had lined up around eighteen to nineteen hours would be realistic. The record at the time was eighteen hours and ten minutes, so I thought 'why not set a schedule for eighteen hours and see how it goes?' I wasn't sure if I could do it in that time, but I was prepared to risk setting off fast so I could see how close I could get to the record. On previous rounds I had wasted over forty minutes sitting down between sections; this time I was determined to reduce this to ten minutes and thus immediately save half an hour.

At 5.30 a.m. on 26 August 2006, I set off from Llanberis on a clockwise round. I completed the first two sections in a fast five hours and twenty minutes. On the next climb up Moel Siabod it all started to go wrong. I seemed to have no strength in my legs; I was climbing really slowly. You always go through bad spells on these long rounds and I was hoping that this was the case here. So I ate as much as I could, but I was not confident that it would help. It seemed to be a lack of strength in the legs rather than a lack of energy. The support team were looking worried and I could see they were wondering why I was going so slowly. Eventually we reached the top and as soon as we started to go downhill I was able to go a decent speed, however the damage had been done. When we got down to Aberglaslyn I was one hour behind schedule. I had been working really hard over the previous section and had still lost time – I knew the record was out of my reach and I was quite depressed. Not only was the record out of reach but I had another eight to nine hours of hard work to go in order to actually finish the round.

I struggled badly climbing Moel Hebog. The bottom section was deep grass and bracken and every step seemed hard work. I was now using walking poles, which took some of the effort off my tired legs, but these were probably more of a help psychologically than in reality. At this stage everything started to hurt, and it still seemed such a long way to go. It was very hard mentally and I was wondering why I was doing it and why I wanted to put myself through such pain. At times I felt like crying. My support team of Helene Whitaker (née Diamantides – one of Britain's best-ever mountain runners) and Welsh fell-running friend Adam Haynes kept talking and encouraging me and got me through my dark points. Eventually we were descending to Pont Cae Gors and then on to the final section. It was dark and with another five hours to go, but I was suddenly a lot happier – I was on the final major climb with running friend and husband of Helene, Jonathan Whitaker, supporting me. I was going to finish this round, it was just a matter of plodding onwards.

Coming off Snowdon I started to feel really sick; if I had eaten or drunk anything I am pretty sure I would have thrown it back up. Luckily there were only a few little climbs left. I finished at 1.57 a.m. after twenty hours and twenty-seven minutes, currently the ninth fastest. (Tim Higginbottom holds the men's record of seventeen hours and forty-two minutes, and Jasmin Paris the women's of eighteen hours and thirty-three minutes.) I had completed the third of the big three rounds and joined the group of thirty-seven people to have done all three, and currently in the fifth-fastest cumulative time. However, in the back of my mind I was disappointed not to have got closer to the record when I have the potential to do it.

Looking back at my report ten days after finishing I wrote '*Strangely I feel very different to the previous rounds. This time I have felt light headed and feverish but the legs do not seem too tired. Previous times I have had no strength in my legs but I have had a clear head. I am very happy to have completed the round and although there were many times whilst out that I was not enjoying it, the sense of achievement outweighs all those negatives.*'

Thinking about my recovery from these long rounds I find that if I eat and drink well all the way round I tend to recover quite quickly. On the Ramsay Round I ate very little over the second ten hours and so by the time the Paddy Buckley Round came I was still not fully recovered, which would explain why I struggled so much.

While I was running my family had a good time in Liverpool being looked after by Emma's sister, Anne, and her husband, Stephen, even if James did keep on saying 'I not want Dada to go for a long run'. There is nothing quite like a child to make you understand the selfish attitude needed to complete these long runs. I try to spend as much time as possible with my family but if I did not go running I could certainly be with them more. I am very fortunate to be married to Emma, who is willing to let me go out running and enjoy my selfish pursuits.

05   2008 LAKELAND 100

The Lakeland 100 is a 105-mile (169-kilometre) race around the Lake District, starting and finishing at Coniston and generally going over the passes rather than the summits. (There is also the Lakeland 50 race which runs simultaneously over the second half of the Lakeland 100 course.) The route goes via the Duddon, Eskdale, Wasdale and Buttermere valleys before arriving in Keswick. From here the route heads round Ullswater and continues over to Haweswater before returning via Kentmere, Ambleside and Elterwater to the finish at Coniston. In each valley there is a checkpoint and all have a plentiful supply of food and friendly marshals. There are about 6,900 metres of ascent and a real mixture of terrain varying from fell, good tracks, to roads – about sixteen kilometres of the race is on roads.

I entered the first running of the Lakeland 100, which started on 8 August 2008. At 7.30 p.m. thirty-one people set off. Soon I was in the lead using my poles to get a good speed up the Walna Scar Road. Once I started descending I extended my lead and for the rest of the race I didn't see another competitor. It was a great starry night and I enjoy being out alone on a night like that. I was also feeling really strong, running up gentle hills without much effort. But the downhills were all sore as I had a bruised heel that seemed to be getting worse. Dawn came as I approached the Blencathra Centre and the clouds were starting to build up – the forecast of heavy rain and wind looked to be pretty accurate. The next section to Dockray passed within a mile of my new house near Threlkeld, and I had thought I could give up here if the pain in my heel got too much. But it seemed to get better (or maybe everything else was beginning to hurt more!).

I reached Dockray (the halfway point in the original route used only in the first running of this race) and the resupply point, where a bag that was handed in before the start was waiting for us, after eleven hours and ten minutes. After a ten-minute break to change shoes and socks and eat some more food I set off with a target of twelve hours and forty minutes for the second half in order to break twenty-four hours. The weather turned really nasty as I descended to Haweswater but I was still feeling strong although everything was sore on the descents. But a mile before the Ambleside checkpoint I hit a very bad patch. After lots of soup and tea at the checkpoint I felt strong enough for the next section to Chapel Stile (although it was a bit of a fight through the crowds and cars of Ambleside at the start of the section). Mistakenly I thought that I had nearly finished, but it was still over twenty-four kilometres and four hours to go! I plodded on keen to finish it off as soon as possible and still with twenty-four hours in my mind. I finally knew I could do the twenty-four hours when I got to Tilberthwaite, though I didn't realise how big the last hill was! Eventually I was back in Coniston to win the race in twenty-three hours and forty minutes. The marshals did a great job of feeding me and I went to bed in my nearby tent extremely tired and sore, but happy. Through the night the weather got worse and I could hear the thunder but also the occasional cheers of the marshals as there was another finisher. In the end only eleven out of the thirty-one finished the race.

06 2009 LAKE DISTRICT TWENTY-FOUR-HOUR RECORD ATTEMPT

Once Alan Heaton had completed the Bob Graham Round he and his brother Ken started to see how it could be extended and how many peaks could be achieved in twenty-four hours. They succeeded in increasing the number of peaks and were followed in their record breaking by Eric Beard and then Joss Naylor. Joss Naylor's record of seventy-two peaks in 1975 was thought by many people to be unbeatable. But in 1988 Mark McDermott extended the number of peaks to seventy-six and in 1997 Mark Hartell added another peak to increase the record to seventy-seven. The distance corresponds to approximately one and a half Bob Graham Rounds, so equates to doing a Bob Graham Round in sixteen hours and then carrying on at the same speed for another eight hours. After supporting someone else on a leg of their Bob Graham Round I was hoping to support Mark Hartell on his successful attempt in 1997, but he was up on his schedule, so by the time I had turned up at Dunmail Raise he had just gone through and I had missed the opportunity to help him.

What was interesting when talking to the two Marks was their attention to detail. They knew the route perfectly and had a very precise schedule that they had remembered, so during the attempt they knew exactly how long it was meant to take between each of the tops. The road crossings were also carefully organised so they did not stop. There was a tray of food and they just grabbed what was needed on the way through. In addition to the standard support team, on each section they had also arranged for extra supporters to carry food and drink up to carefully selected locations so the main support team did not need to carry much and could therefore keep up with them. So in my opinion, although they were slower runners than Joss, they made up for it with planning and preparation so they could beat Joss's record.

In 2009 I set myself the challenge of having a go at breaking this record. This is a very different sort of challenge from the Lakeland 100. It is not a race where the aim is to finish as fast as possible but an all or nothing attempt to break a record. When you start something like this you need to decide what to do if the record becomes impossible. It is a difficult decision. You can carry on and finish in over twenty-four hours, but there is no record or recognition for the amazing effort and commitment. Or, you can drop out and accept that on the day for whatever reason the record is impossible and you can save some energy for the rest of the season. It is not really a decision you want to think about before you start because as soon as you contemplate failure it becomes more likely. But in the back of my mind I decided that if the record became unattainable then I would probably drop out. Unlike a Bob Graham Round there is no spare time in the schedule to make up more than a few minutes; an hour or so is definitely impossible to regain.

Over the spring of 2009 I spent many hours running over the route. On most Saturdays I was up at dawn and would go for a four-hour run before returning home and helping look after the family. One day over Easter I completed forty per cent (equivalent to sixty per cent of the Bob Graham Round) of the route in ten hours. I also found a slightly better route than Mark Hartell through the Langdale Pikes down into Langdale and back up to Pike o' Blisco. This saved me about ten minutes. So on 23 May I was ready and I set off at 3 a.m. hoping to break the record.

The weather looked a bit wet to start with but was forecast to dry up by the afternoon. After four hours in the Northern Fells I had got to Threlkeld but I was twenty minutes down on schedule despite running strongly. Unfortunately the previous week was really wet and underfoot conditions on this grassy/peaty section were really slow and sapping. I tried really hard (probably too hard) over the next section to Dunmail and only lost a couple more minutes. After that I started to suffer and never really recovered, so that at Wasdale after sixteen hours and fifty peaks I was one and a half hours down on schedule and I decided to give up. There was no way I could have caught that up. I could probably have carried on and done around seventy peaks, but the nice weather forecast for the afternoon had not materialised and with fifty-kilometre-per-hour winds and drizzle on the tops I didn't really feel like carrying on for another eight hours. Stopping was a really hard decision, particularly as I had a strong support team waiting for the next section and I felt like I was letting them down. But I had the chance to have another go the next year, where I would hopefully be fitter and even better prepared.

07   2009 LAKELAND 100

Later in 2009 I decided to try to defend the Lakeland 100 title. I had done a really good year of training for the Lake District twenty-four-hour record and was definitely fitter and stronger than the previous year. I knew it would be hard as many of the UK's top ultrarunners were present. However, with a wet night and cool weather forecast – my favourite – I was confident I could do it.

At 7.30 p.m. on 31 July, about 120 competitors set off from Coniston (on a slightly different route to the previous year, missing out a section early on but adding a bit in the middle near Dalemain). I tried to hold back to start with but by the time we reached Seathwaite, Andy Rankin, the top UK ultrarunner in that year, and I had a decent lead. We ran together for the next section but he got away just before Boot. I enjoyed the next two sections past Burnmoor Tarn to Wasdale and then over Black Sail and Scarth Gap to Buttermere. I was going steadily but strongly and happy to be out in the rain and dark over proper Lake District fells. So when I reached Buttermere I was surprised that Andy was seven minutes in front of me. I eventually managed to catch up with him over the next section so that we reached Braithwaite together. We ran together and chatted to the Blencathra Centre and could not see anyone in sight on this big loop, so realised we must have at least a forty-minute lead.

The next section to Dockray goes very near to where I live so navigation was not a problem but I was beginning to suffer on the hard trails; everything was stiffening up in my quads and pelvic region. The last few kilometres to the resupply point at Dalemain were on roads and although I was running at a decent speed it was getting painful. Andy got ahead here; I took a bit longer changing my shoes and socks and getting my trekking poles out. I hoped the poles would help and by using my arms and shoulders I was keeping a reasonable pace uphill, but I was beginning to suffer badly. I eventually caught Andy descending to Haweswater, after I found a good line through the bracken. We stayed together to Mardale and then to the top of the Gatescarth Pass. As we started descending I was OK on the steep section but as the descent flattened off my legs refused to work any more. My quads seemed to have locked solid. Suddenly I was no longer racing just fighting to get to the finish and with six hours or so to go I didn't know how I was going to manage that. I didn't know if I could push myself through that sort of suffering for that length of time. I decided to focus on each section and to try and reach the next checkpoint.

I got to Kentmere, then Ambleside and to Chapel Stile. But I was going slower and slower and putting in loads of effort yet still losing time to Andy. By Chapel Stile he had a thirty-minute lead. I was trying to run the flats but it was barely faster than a walk – it was the classic Bob Graham Round shuffle. Five minutes after Chapel Stile I could take no more. Physically and mentally I had had enough. I put my waterproof on and sat on the grass for ten minutes. I had decided to give up; the question was how I would get back to Coniston. The fastest route was just about the way I was going, just missing out the final climb. So I got up and started walking, very slowly, to Tilberthwaite. After an hour of walking I was bored and I was feeling a bit better so I started to jog. Eventually I stopped feeling sorry for myself, I was in second place and that would be a result worth having so I decided to finish. As soon as I recovered mentally I felt better physically and I began moving OK. I actually enjoyed the final climb out of Tilberthwaite and the big descent back into Coniston. I finally finished in twenty-four hours and five minutes. This was twenty-five minutes slower than the previous year and well over an hour behind Andy.

I was really disappointed with my run but I had learnt a big lesson. I had started with the wrong mental attitude; I had set off trying to win the race and I was not focused on looking after myself. As soon as I realised that I was not going to win, for the first time in my life I completely lost it mentally. I still find it hard to admit that I gave up and sat down. I always say that feeling tired and having a bad run is not an excuse to stop but I did. Although I eventually carried on I was no longer racing just finishing. The problem was I had been determined to win and once that was impossible I could no longer take the pain and so I gave up. I should have set off with the attitude of completing the route as fast as possible and not have been worried about anyone else's race. The key to these long races is pacing and nutrition, basically looking after yourself, but if you race against someone else you can forget these and the consequences are very painful.

08 2010 LAKE DISTRICT TWENTY-FOUR-HOUR RECORD ATTEMPT

A great thing about fell running is that there is a tradition of record holders helping people break their existing records. So in 2010, when I had another attempt at the Lake District twenty-four-hour record, I was very happy to be supported by both Mark McDermott and Mark Hartell, the existing and previous record holders.

I set off at 3 a.m. on 19 June and this time the weather was perfect. The day was dry, but not too hot and with light winds. After a dry couple of months, underfoot conditions were also perfect for a fast time. The first section over the Northern Fells went well, I was running strongly and keeping on schedule. However, after Threlkeld on the climb up to Clough Head my stomach felt really bloated – it was swollen and sore. All the food and drink seemed to be sitting there and not being absorbed. Thinking about it I reckoned I had probably been having too many gels, energy drinks and sweet food, but very little water. With a support team running with me and offering me food I made the stupid mistake of taking too much on board. Despite eating less and drinking mainly water the bloating just remained. With a northerly wind and travelling south along the Helvellyn range I still kept on schedule on this section and on the section to Langdale I was only a few minutes down.

However, after this I was struggling badly, my bloated stomach was getting more painful and I was losing minutes on every section. It was hard knowing the record was slipping away from me, but there was nothing I could do about it. Eventually climbing Esk Pike my stomach had had enough and everything came back up quite violently. After being sick I suddenly felt lighter and I ran up Great End really quickly. But I quickly ran out of energy and struggled on the rest of the section to Wasdale Head, eventually arriving there about an hour behind schedule. This time I carried on but I lost lots more time on my schedule up Yewbarrow and Red Pike. Soon after that I realised my chance of breaking the record was definitely gone and I sat down on a rock and told my support team that I was giving up. We gently walked to Honister Pass and let everyone know what had happened.

To have failed twice to break this record was really hard. I put a lot of time and effort into being perfectly prepared, I spent a lot of time out training away from my young family and both times I pushed it to my limit but it was not good enough. People say you learn more from your failures than your successes, but most of the important stuff I knew already. Firstly, this is an amazingly good record and very much at the limit of what I am capable of. Secondly, sometimes the weather makes things impossible. Thirdly, nutrition is essential to completing these rounds. However, getting nutrition correct is so hard. The frequency of a record attempt like this is at best once a year, so testing what works is really difficult. Afterwards I went through a great period of self-doubt. I wondered if I was good enough to win races and break records, and at forty-two years old I was only likely to get slower.

09   2012 BERGHAUS DRAGON'S BACK RACE

The legendary Dragon's Back Race was first run in 1992. The five-day race takes competitors down the mountainous spine of Wales from Conwy on the north coast to Carreg Cennen Castle close to the south coast. The total distance is around 300 kilometres with about 17,000 metres of ascent. It is classed as one of the world's toughest races because not only is it a long way every day, it also passes through wild, remote and mostly trackless ground.

Helene Diamantides and Martin Stone won the first race with sixteen of the thirty-two pairs who started completing the course. In 2012, Shane Ohly (director of Ourea Events and winner of the OMM elite class) decided to put the event on again and I was desperate to have a go. The idea of running the length of Wales in five days with mountains, rough ground and navigation between tops is such a great concept. Berghaus were also happy to take me on as one of their athletes and support me for the race. The only problem was taking a week away from home, particularly as the race was the start of September and so Hannah's first ever week of school. However, Emma was happy for me to do it, so I had a great challenge for the year.

Once I had entered, the reality of running sixty kilometres with around 3,000 metres of ascent each day for five consecutive days dawned on me. I find that sort of distance in a single day or two days is no problem, but five days is a big deal and I was nervous. I knew looking after my body on the first few days would be crucial; any rubbing, niggles etc. would just get worse and worse, making finishing impossible or extremely painful. I hoped that I could be running nearly as fast on the last day as the first.

Having learnt from previous races and mistakes, my aim for the race was firstly to have a good time and finish it (I needed to make sure I ran my own race and not try to race other competitors). Secondly, I wanted to do well, but as I am a competitive person that will automatically happen, I will always push it to see how fast I can go.

I arrived in Conwy the day before it started after a relaxing drive down with Helene Diamantides. I had a hotel room in Llandudno, which was great as it was away from all the other competitors and their stresses and anxieties. I spent a couple of hours sorting out my kit then went off to register and go to the race briefing and a talk by Martin Stone about the race twenty years ago. Registration and the briefing were very smooth and I felt relaxed and excited. Shane Ohly told us that we were doing a longer day one and a shorter day five than in 1992. But I knew the course was different from twenty years ago, all that mattered was doing the course I was given as fast as possible. More importantly he said that on the first day we were doing the Welsh 3,000s (every 3,000-foot peak in Wales). This meant a lot of ridge running and not much water, and with a hot day forecast it was already clear that hydration would be important.

At 7 a.m. the next morning we left Conwy Castle to start the race. We had dropped off our bags forty minutes earlier. In those forty minutes I drank another bottle of water. I also needed the toilet but I had a bit of a sneaky plan – the timing only started at the end of the castle walls. I sprinted off at 7 a.m. on the sound of the starting gun and went straight to the visitor centre toilets. I joined the rest of the competitors at the back and so started a couple of minutes after the fastest runners. After about thirty minutes I had caught up with the leading guys. I felt great and I had a couple of minutes' lead on them as I officially started two minutes after them! So I continued at a fast (probably too fast) pace – I didn't want everyone following me all day. We passed a stream before the first checkpoint; I drank my water, filled my bottle up and splashed some more over my head.

By the time we reached the third checkpoint I had slowed down a little and let the three guys just behind catch up. With me were Rob Baker, Mark Palmer and Jim Mann (Jim won the next race in 2015 and holds the winter Bob Graham Round record) – three of the guys that I knew were potential winners of the race. Rob and Mark had been beating me in fell races all year. Jim struggled on the contouring leg to Yr Elen so on the final peak (Pen Yr Ole Wen) before Llyn Ogwen there were just three of us. We decided to take the easterly route as it was gentler and had a stream part way down. We reached the bag drop together. It was really hot down there, and the marshals sprayed us with water and also gave us water to drink. I had two litres to drink, filled my water bottle, grabbed my food bag and was off first. Luckily I found the tourist path up Tryfan and as I climbed I started to feel stronger as the food and drink got into my system. I reached the summit with no sign of Rob and Mark – they had chosen another, slower way. Coming off Tryfan I was cramping up but I was taking electrolyte tablets so I thought it wouldn't get any worse. I couldn't see the path to the top of Glyder Fach so I just went up the Bristly Ridge (a grade-one scramble), which was quite enjoyable with the dry rock, even though I am not a rock climber. The ridge along to Eldir Fawr I had done before on my Paddy Buckley Round, but there was more climbing than I had remembered.

When I reached the summit I looked back and could see someone around twenty minutes behind me. I ran along the ridge a bit further and found some nice scree and then a path down to the road at the bottom. It was a couple of kilometres along the Llanberis Pass road and the major climb up to Crib Goch. There was a nice river on the climb to keep me cool and hydrated. But I was struggling and climbing slowly. I was not sure of the way up, but eventually I could see the col between Crib Goch and Garnedd Ugain and I headed for that. I was getting very wobbly at this stage and only climbing at around ten metres per minute, but I pushed on hard. Eventually I reached the col and continued along the ridge to the summit. I had never been on Crib Goch before and although I knew it was rocky, I was surprised by how difficult it was. I tried following the ridge but had to retrace my steps a couple of times when I reached some big drops. I quickly realised the best route was off to the south side of the ridge. Eventually I reached the checkpoint and could see Rob Baker just below me coming up the north ridge. This spurred me into action and I returned to the col along a much better line and up to the summit of Snowdon. I passed Mark Palmer on the way as he had taken a bad route choice to Crib Goch. I was shattered but luckily I can descend quite fast however tired I am. The descent was long but eventually I reached the road and the last kilometre to the finish of day one. I was completely exhausted but I knew refuelling as soon as possible was vitally important. I was weighed as part of a nutrition study and I had lost four and a half kilograms – I clearly needed to get a lot of fluid inside me. I had some tea and soup and lay down on my air mat. I don't really remember much of the next three hours – I tried to drink more and the doctor came round several times to check I was OK. I didn't move much and I was very close to being sick.

After the race I talked to one of the Berghaus guys who thought I had overdone it so much on day one I would have no chance of recovering in time for the next day and so had blown my opportunity to win the race. Rob Baker came in twenty-three minutes down, then Sam Smith about fifty minutes after me, followed by Mark Palmer over an hour behind me. Clearly this tough long day was causing everyone to suffer. Once I had recovered enough I ate as much as I could and then tried to go to sleep in a tent which I shared with Rob. Unfortunately sleep did not really come; as soon as I lay down there was a really bad pain in my knees, lower legs and ankles – the pain moving all the time but always sore. The caffeine I had been taking all afternoon also seemed to keep me awake, but at least I was lying down resting.

By the second morning I was still one kilogram down on my pre-race weight. Clearly I needed to make sure I didn't get dehydrated again.

Luckily the weather that morning was my favourite running conditions – wet and drizzly. I set off with Rob, as the last of the starters. We were both feeling tired, and happy to go steadily to start with. We passed lots of people on Cnicht and more climbing Moelwyn Mawr. But the drizzle stopped at this point and the sun came out. After this it was a long route-choice leg to the bag drop point (or transition point) at Cwm Bychan at the bottom of the Roman Steps on the Rhinogs. I went straight and Rob went a long way east on the road around Lake Trawsfynydd. I was just leaving this transition point when Rob turned up – at which point I had a lead of around three minutes. A big group with Helene was also ten minutes in front and I was keen to catch them as I knew the route on the next section around the Rhinogs was difficult and Helene had reccied some of it. I gradually caught and passed Helene's group and could see my lead on Rob was extending. On the last two summits I pushed hard and then it was just a long descent and a flat road section to the finish. I just about kept a good pace going, and Rob, having taken a few bad route choices, finished twenty-seven minutes after me to give me an overall lead of fifty minutes. Helene had moved up into third place, three hours behind me. Clearly the race was between Rob and me, but we were both very tired and wondering how we could cope with three more long days. This is often the hardest point of any long race, when you are completely exhausted but still not even halfway round. Once you can get over half way the end might not be in sight but it becomes mentally slightly easier.

I had another bad night's sleep and really struggled to think clearly and get prepared for another long day. Rob and I again agreed to set off together. This time we set off slower still and walked the steep climbs on the road. Eventually we reached the fell and had an enjoyable climb and then run along the ridge of Cadair Idris. A long, flatter section followed before a climb up to Tarrenhendre. Here leaning forward to fill my water bottle a grass reed went straight into my eye. This cut my contact lens into two and made my eye a bit sore. I would have to manage with one good eye and one sore eye. Eventually we descended into the town of Machynlleth. The final steep descent and the heat at this low level left me suddenly feeling exhausted. We stopped in the garage for some Coke and a sandwich and continued to the bag drop point. After more food and drink we were off, but it was clear that I was going slower than Rob, so he gradually got away from me. However, a dodgy bit of map enabled me to catch up. After this we stayed nearly together; while Rob was running steadily, I would run fast for 100 metres and then walk. The big climb of Plynlimon was not as bad as I had expected and the first part of the descent from there to the finish was a perfect gentle angle. I finished with Rob, so the positions between us had not changed but we had taken another hour out of Helene and the group around her. That night we camped in a barn, which was a bit rocky but at least we didn't have to worry about dew in the morning.

I woke up the next morning feeling really rough. Muscles everywhere were hurting and my chest was tight. I was planning to start with Rob but I was ready first and shivering. So we agreed it was best that I should leave straight away. For this day I changed shoes from my Inov-8 X-Talons to my Berghaus Vapour Claws. There was a lot of road and track running lined up for the day, so I thought trail shoes would be better. Strangely, as soon as I set off I felt great, I think because it was that bit cooler than on the previous days. I kept looking back but there was no sign of Rob. Maybe he had left a big gap before starting? I couldn't risk going slowly and letting him catch up, I had to go hard – especially with the road sections that I knew Rob would be stronger than me on.

I made a bad route choice and got stuck in some horrible terrain between Esgair Penygarreg and the Elan Village, but Rob had not been through when I arrived. I decided to go on the road to the end of the reservoir. I hate running on roads but I knew it would be faster. The road was as horrible as I thought it was going to be. I was getting a lot of pain down my legs from my lower back and I had a new problem. I was getting really bad tendonitis at the front of my lower left leg just above my ankle. I enjoyed the rest of the day while I was climbing but the descents and the flat road sections were really painful. At least the last eight kilometres on the road were undulating rather than flat, but I was very relieved to see the finish. There was a lovely cool river to swim in, which provided some relief for my leg. Over an hour later, Rob ran in looking very tired; he had had a bad day and my lead was two hours. In most races that sort of lead would be impossible to lose, but not in the Dragon's Back. I knew how sore my leg was, and if I had to walk significant parts of the route I could easily lose those two hours.

On the last day I again set off with Rob. We knew there was no point in racing. The injury was the only thing that would prevent me from winning and similarly there was a three-hour gap behind Rob. We passed a lot of other runners – or walkers by this point in the race – and although I felt sore I knew it was nothing compared with many of these other guys – so it was time to stop whinging and get on with it. After three hours we reached the resupply point with Helene's group, who had set off twenty minutes before us. After this it was a big climb up to 800 metres at Fan Brycheiniog. It was a pleasure walking up this mountain compared to running on the tracks and roads where the pain in my leg was intense. The ridge from there to the final checkpoint at Tair Carn Isaf was great running on another beautiful sunny day. The only problem was the lack of water. Soon we had descended from the final checkpoint to the river and were making our way up the final climb to Carreg Cennen Castle. I sprinted the last climb and crossed the line to win the 2012 Dragon's Back Race.

Overall, it was an amazing experience. Winning was great, but more importantly it was a brilliant journey along the length of Wales over almost all the major peaks. As expected there were some amazing highs during the five days – in particular the views. On the evening of the third day we even had time to stop for a minute on the top of Plynlimon, the highest mountain in that part of Wales, and appreciate these views.

The low points were the feeling of dehydration creeping up on me on a couple of days, and also that getting-up-in-the-morning feeling, thinking about pushing my tired, aching body through another day of running.

The tough nature of the race meant that only thirty-two of the ninety people who started the race finished. For winning I received a brilliant trophy, which used the same mould as the original 1992 trophy. It has a dragon with a range of mountains down its spine. It is very heavy and my children love it and enjoy carrying it around, although I am very worried they will drop it and break their toes. They named it 'Mountain Breath' and Hannah says that as dragons live in caves we need to keep it behind the sofa. I occasionally sneak it out and put it on the mantelpiece before she tells me to put it behind the sofa again!

The morning after the race, the tendonitis was really bad and I could barely hobble. For the next two weeks I was also tired and hungry all the time. But my recovery seemed to be fast and after a couple of weeks the swelling from the tendonitis had gone down and I felt my energy levels were back to normal. So I thought it would be fine to start running again. However, although the tendonitis was OK, running was very painful, I was getting quite a lot of nerve pain in my legs and I was starting to run with a different gait. I stupidly decided to just carry on, and ran in quite a lot of races. Then I decided to enter the OMM with Dave Wilby, who I had previously run with in adventure races. But halfway through the first day my right knee started clicking. Overnight my knee swelled up badly and although I tried to set off on the second day, after a couple of minutes running in agony it was clear I was not going to run this injury off. I had to retire from an OMM for the first time after twenty-two successful completions.

Once the swelling had gone down I realised my kneecap was not tracking correctly and the muscles above my knee were completely unbalanced. It was obvious that I would need a long time off and lots of work gradually building up the appropriate muscles. This was my first long rest from running since I was twenty and I was much better at coping than in those days. Work and children certainly kept me busy.

Eventually after six months I was back to running properly. Unfortunately Rob struggled even more than me in the aftermath of the Dragon's Back Race. He needed a heart operation and had to take two years off from any serious running.

2 Considering the Challenge

10 THE WAINWRIGHTS

Alfred Wainwright (1907–1991) was born in Blackburn, Lancashire, but moved to Kendal in 1941 to be closer to the Lake District fells and he lived there for the rest of his life. His seven-volume *Pictorial Guide to the Lakeland Fells* was published between 1955 and 1966, although he started to write them in 1952. The books have encouraged generations of people on to the fells and have now sold millions of copies. The 214 fells described in the seven books have become known as the Wainwrights. The highest of the Wainwrights is England's highest mountain, Scafell Pike (978 metres), and the smallest is Castle Crag in Borrowdale (298 metres). They stretch over a distance of forty-two kilometres from east to west and thirty-nine kilometres from north to south. Each fell has its own chapter in his books, which describes the summit and surrounding area in detail, including beautiful three-dimensional drawings of the various routes to the summit. Alfred Wainwright also wrote an additional book called *The Outlying Fells of Lakeland*, which describes another 116 fells around the edge of the Lake District.

'Peak bagging' in the UK is really popular, with people spending many years attempting to climb a set of summits. Probably the most well known are the 282 Scottish mountains over 3,000 feet (914 metres) called the Munros. Climbing to the top of all of these hills – 'Munro bagging' – is an ambition for many people, which normally takes many years or decades to achieve. The 214 Wainwrights are the most popular Lake District set and are much more attainable than the Munros. A list is maintained by the Long Distance Walkers Association (LDWA) of people who have

THERE IS NO MAP IN HELL

registered as having completed all the Wainwrights.[1] This number stood at 759 at end of 2016, but there are many people who have completed the Wainwrights who have not registered. There are other important sets of fells in the Lake District covering many of the same tops but also some others. There are 114 Lake District Hewitts, which are tops over 2,000 feet (610 metres) with at least a thirty-metre drop on all sides. Fifty-five Marilyns are specified in the Lake District, where a Marilyn can be any height as long as there is a drop of at least 150 metres on all sides. There are also 171 Lake District Nuttalls – a list of hills and mountains maintained by John and Anne Nuttall, and detailed in *The Mountains of England and Wales* published by Cicerone Press. Finally, there are 541 Lake District Birketts – Lake District hills over 1,000 feet (305 metres) listed in Bill Birkett's *Complete Lakeland Fells*.

Another important thing about the Wainwrights is that they will never change – there will always be 214 Wainwrights with the summits in the places specified by Wainwright. These can be a bit odd and quirky; they are sometimes not the highest point of a fell but a nearby smaller top with a better view. Whereas, for the Munros and other summits specified by heights there are changes in the lists as the tops are measured more accurately. These changes make it difficult when trying to set a record or fastest known time (FKT) as the criteria will have changed. However, for the Wainwrights, there will never be any changes, so the FKT is a well-defined record.

---

1. *www.ldwa.org.uk/hillwalkers/register2.php*

11 WAINWRIGHT RUNNERS: BLAND, HEATON AND NAYLOR

Once Wainwright had published his guidebooks, walkers started to attempt to reach the summits of all 214 Wainwright fells. The challenge was to complete them all rather than do it as fast as possible. But that soon changed, first with Chris Bland in 1981, followed by Alan Heaton in 1985 and Joss Naylor in 1986. These are three legendary fell runners, and they each attempted fast runs of all 214 Wainwright fells.

Chris Bland was from Borrowdale and he was a great runner although not as fast or well known as the other Blands, his cousins, from the same valley – Billy, David and Stuart. I knew Chris for many years as we were both members of the West Cumberland Orienteering Club. He was a great guy and I always enjoyed chatting to him. He also made the best-ever trophies out of local stone and I was lucky enough to win some over the years; they are still proudly displayed in my house. In 1981 he had a go at doing a Wainwright book each day for seven consecutive days, and as he was raising money for the church roof in Borrowdale he started and finished each day at a church.[1] In the usual fell-runner's understatement,

---

1. On the first day Chris completed the thirty-five eastern fells in sixteen hours and twenty-nine minutes. On the second day he attempted the thirty-six far-eastern fells but stopped at Troutbeck church after thirteen hours and eighteen minutes and twenty-seven tops. He struggled with a lack of food and although he reckons he could have completed it he was worried about completing the next day. On the third day he completed the twenty-seven central fells in thirteen hours and twenty-seven minutes. On the fourth day he attempted the thirty southern fells, which includes Scafell and Scafell Pike. However, it was a really misty, windy day and in the end he completed seventeen tops in twelve hours and forty minutes. After that he managed to complete a book a day. Day five was the northern fells and he completed twenty-four tops in fourteen hours and forty-eight minutes. Day six was the north-western fells and he completed twenty-nine tops in fifteen hours and fifty-eight minutes. On day seven he completed the thirty-two western fells in nineteen hours and forty-seven minutes.

he wrote in a pamphlet entitled *Seven Books in Seven Days* that 'For any-one in Britain, any of the books in twenty-four hours represents a real challenge. That I failed to complete the entire programme no longer worries me. Before the event I was so terrified of failing miserably, that when things went so well, this was the greatest mental and physical boost I could have hoped for. I learnt much on days two and four, the latter being the worst for weather. These two days give someone else room to improve on my performance.' I remember ten years after his amazing achievement his pamphlet was printed over the course of a year in the West Cumberland Orienteering Club bimonthly magazine. Reading it at the time I found it very inspiring and amazing that someone could run so far in a single day, let alone day after day for a week.

Unfortunately Chris suffered from depression during and after the Foot and Mouth crisis of 2001. He died in March 2003, a sad loss for the Borrowdale valley and the fell running and orienteering communities.

I don't think I have ever met Alan Heaton. However, his achievements are amazing and he has inspired me and many other runners over the years. He is member number one in the Bob Graham Club (I am number 1,244) – the first person to complete the Bob Graham Round after Bob himself, in 1960 in a time of twenty-two hours and eighteen minutes.[2] He extended this round on several occasions to hold the Lake District twenty-four-hour record with a best of sixty peaks in 1965 with a time of twenty-three hours and thirty-four minutes. He also did sixty-four peaks in 1974 but was thirty minutes over the allowed twenty-four hours. Overall, Alan made three successful and nine unsuccessful attempts at the Lake District twenty-four-hour record.[3] On 29 June 1985 at 3 a.m., twenty-five years after he first completed the Bob Graham Round, he set out to complete a Wainwrights round starting and finishing at Keswick

---

2. *www.bobgrahamclub.org.uk*
3. *Stud Marks on the Summits*, 411–413.

Moot Hall. He decided not to consider which of the Wainwright books the fells were described in but to join all 214 tops up in the best way for a continuous traverse. By the fourth day he was beginning to suffer with his feet: 'The descent from Clough Head was in the full heat of the after-noon sun and my feet felt like they were on fire by the time I got to Wanthwaite. When my shoes were removed it proved to be more than the heat that was causing the pain. The fourth toe of my left foot was swollen and very tender.' Later that day he says, 'The thought crossed my mind that this might be the beginning of the end'. On the fifth day he went to Keswick hospital to get a course of antibiotics, so he did not start day five until 12.50 p.m. By day nine he was having real problems with his feet: 'I was still climbing well but the downhills were very painful and traversing the worst of all'. On the tenth day his feet were getting really bad and he says, 'Whilst traversing Causey my feet gave me so much pain that I flopped into the wet grass for a few minutes to regain my compo-sure'. He finished at 8.12 p.m. on 8 July after nine days, sixteen hours and forty-two minutes. He notes there were 'not many people around'.

Following the fell-running tradition, other top fell runners of the era helped him. Chris Bland supported him on the fells for a couple of sections, and he also stayed in a caravan parked at Chris and Sheila Bland's house on several nights and on another night he stayed at Joss and Mary Naylor's house.

He concludes in the pamphlet he wrote entitled *The Wainwright Round* that 'I would say that the twenty-five years of endeavour on the hills has brought me much frustration and disappointment but these are far outweighed by the rewards I have had. These come in different forms. Some comes from having the help and companionship of many willing people who have given a large amount of time and effort in supporting me, and some from the satisfaction which stems from testing yourself and succeeding in mastering your fallibilities in an environment where you like to be.'

Joss Naylor MBE is the most famous fell runner in the UK. A man known as 'Iron Joss' because of his legendary exploits and his ability to carry on however tired and however much he is suffering. He is a complete inspiration to me and loads of other fell runners. He has broken the Lake District twenty-four-hour record three times, including completing seventy-two peaks in 1975 in twenty-three hours and eleven minutes. Other records he has broken include the Pennine Way and the Welsh 3,000s. He has also won the Ennerdale Horseshoe fell race nine times in a row, and has ten victories at the Lake District Mountain Trial.

I know Joss fairly well and I still see him, now in his eighties, out on the fells helping his son gather in the sheep. He also regularly helps out at fell races giving out the prizes or giving out water on the longer races such as the Wasdale Fell Race, which passes next to his house. It is interesting to note that when Alan Heaton claimed a record, Joss would often come along a year or two later and beat it. The Wainwright fells record is no exception – Alan made his attempt in 1985 and a year later Joss had a go. He set off at 4 a.m. on 26 June 1986 from Keswick Moot Hall. He chose a similar route to Alan, with the order of the tops best suited to a continuous circuit, but with some modifications to Alan's route. The weather started off really hot and over the course of the next four days this caused Joss to really struggle. In his account of the week, *Joss Naylor MBE was Here*, the level of suffering that Joss encountered is easy to appreciate: 'Such great heat would drive me and my support team so close to submission. During the period we had to drag from ourselves not only our accumulated fitness and basic strength, we had to reach even deeper into ourselves when natural physical abilities had been drained, deeper than I had ever had to reach.' But early on in the week he also had some great times such as sitting in a river at the end of the first day drinking a beer where he comments, 'Happy days'.

His love of the fells shines through the whole of his account. Talking about climbers, fell runners or walkers, 'our bond is the love for these beautiful hills', or 'the finest sunrise I've ever seen in my life, views so good you could almost identify the smit mark on the sheep across the valley'. He even rescued a lamb on the third day.

However, despite his love of the fells, his increase in suffering over the week in his account is obvious. By the second day he already had blisters and these gradually got worse over the following days. By the latter part of the fourth day his legs were heavy, his shoulders tight, the pace had slowed right down and towards the very end of the day he was stumbling at little more than a walk. On the fifth day his support team were cutting bits of his shoes away to relieve the pressure on his ankles, which he says were 'swollen and skinned'. By the sixth day his face, mouth and hands were swollen, and even sipping water was painful. All food had to be liquefied before he could get it down his throat. On the last day it was wet and windy and he had to rely more and more on his support team. By the end he was even having trouble talking, because his mouth was so sore, and the pace had become a walk not a run. However, he showed his toughness and made it back to Keswick and finished with his support team watching as he touched the Moot Hall seven days, one hour and twenty-five minutes after starting out. His wife, Mary, was first to congratulate him.

As well as his written account in *Joss Naylor MBE was Here*, Ken Ledward recorded a fifty-minute audio cassette tape of Joss recounting the entire week, just a week after he finished. I have been very lucky to borrow this tape from Ken and it was an amazing experience to be the first person to hear the words spoken by Joss in twenty-eight years. There are some happy moments, such as on day five when Joss says, 'Who was on the summit of High Raise? Chris Bland and his tin of macaroni pudding. I enjoyed that, great stuff, Chris. There should be more of it on the summits.' However, Joss's levels of suffering feel even more intense and raw in this audio account compared to his written account. At the end of day six he says, 'The cold was in my bones as I dropped into Kirkstile car park. I lost my body heat. I was shivering and I needed something warm inside, which was a terrible job to get down. My mouth at this stage, I couldn't chew with it, I couldn't move anything round it, my tongue inside my mouth was absolutely red raw. I forced a bit of liquid down.' The quiet reception he received when he returned successfully to Keswick can be heard in the following: ' ... along the road back to Keswick where our full team joined in as we walked along the road. There was not a lot said. There were two or three drunks coming out of Keswick having been to an all-night party. They were full of spirits but our spirits were in a small room. When we got to the finish, a welcome bottle of Guinness then back in the van to Ken's.'

12   THE PLAN

The plan was a simple one: I would have a go at running over all 214 Wainwright fells as fast as possible. Like Joss Naylor, and Alan Heaton before him, I planned to start and finish in Keswick, and I too would not worry about which of the seven Wainwright books the fells were from but complete a logical circuit of all 214.

The seed was initially planted in my head by Jo Scott, one of my support team during my first Lake District twenty-four-hour record attempt. Immediately I thought it sounded like a good idea and gradually as I recovered from the Dragon's Back Race the idea appealed to me more and more. I had been over most of the 214 tops, but fifteen of them I had never been up, so it was a great opportunity to complete the Wainwrights. I also liked the simplicity of the challenge. The Wainwright fells are very well known, so wanting to run all 214 as fast as possible is easy for anyone who walks and runs in the Lake District to understand.

As well as climb all 214 fells as fast as possible I wanted to enjoy myself in the process. A week running round the fells with my friends, what could be better? I love being in the fells, running over them and being out at all times of the day and night. I wanted to have a go at Joss Naylor's record but I wasn't sure if I was good enough, and to start with this intention and then fail would be awful – as I had learned from my disappointments at the Lakeland 100. So the plan I told everyone was that my main aim was to climb all 214 Wainwright fells as fast as possible. However, in the back of my mind I was desperate to have a go at Joss's record, but this had to be a secondary objective.

Chris Bland, Billy Bland, Mark McDermott and Mark Hartell had all told me that Joss's pacing for ultraruns was not good. He would set off at nearly full race speed and carry on pushing it as hard as he could for as long as possible, gradually slowing down, until by the end he was sometimes going quite slowly. This was good news for me. I know I am not as fast a runner as Joss was. He only weighs about fifty-seven kilograms (nine stone) whereas my race weight is seventy-three kilograms (eleven stone seven pounds) and it is very difficult to run uphill as fast carrying that extra sixteen kilograms. Looking at fell times, he has won the Ennerdale Fell Race on nine occasions with a best time of around three hours and thirty minutes, whereas I have only once managed it under four hours. He has also won the Lake District Mountain Trial ten times, and I have won it once. So I hoped I would slow down less than Joss over the week.

However, having read the accounts of Chris, Alan and Joss I knew that even finishing was going to be exceptionally hard. I reckoned the route was just over five Bob Graham Rounds distance-wise, but a bit less than five Bob Graham Rounds ascent-wise. So mentally I equated it to five Bob Graham Rounds in less than seven days. Taking into account that I needed sleep, this meant that when I was moving I needed to be going on average at nearly twenty-four-hour Bob Graham Round pace. This was going to be a massive undertaking that came with a considerable chance that I would not break the record, or even complete the challenge. It was a proper challenge.

As well as the difficulty of the run I also needed to think about my family. To stand a chance of completing the challenge would mean getting everything right. There would be many days spent working out the best route, evenings and weekends on the fells selecting the best lines, extra hours and days out training, sorting out all my support team and gear and then the week itself and the aftermath. It would mean being away from my family a lot. I would miss fun days out with the children, bedtimes, relaxing evenings watching TV – normal things that families do.

My family means everything to me, and missing time with them for a selfish pursuit was a really hard decision to make. I also knew how hard it would be on Emma – she would be helping me, looking after our three children and the house, and working. It would mean a massive commitment from her as well as me, but Emma was positive about me having a go – she knows how much running means to me and was happy for me to try.

13   ADDITIONAL MOTIVATION

I am only one year and five months older than my sister Hilary, while Karen and Julian are around five and four years older than me. So I am much closer in age to Hilary and as a child, and in particular as a teenager, I saw a lot more of her than Karen and Julian. Hilary was a very good hockey player at school and at university did lots of rowing. She did some running after leaving university, including completing the London Marathon.

Around ten years ago Hilary was diagnosed with multiple sclerosis (MS). This condition affects nerves in the brain and spinal cord, and causes a wide range of symptoms including problems with muscle movement, balance and vision. For Hilary the main problem seems to be in one leg which means she struggles to walk without a stick and for any distance needs to be in a wheelchair. It's really hard seeing someone so young and previously physically active, struggling to even walk around her own house. I know it is really hard for her but whenever I see Hilary she manages to hide how tough it is and the way her positive attitude shines through is amazing.

To start with she seemed to have relapses or 'flare-ups' of the symptoms quite regularly but without a full recovery during the remission stage. More recently she has been more stable. This appears to be due to the improved drugs that are becoming available and the treatment she has been receiving at the Samson Centre in Surrey near where she lives.

Hilary: 'As someone who was always physically active (OK, maybe not to my brother's level …) the onset of a disease that robs me of that ability is tough to take, but being able to push myself to the new limits my body has set is important to me. What the Samson Centre gives me is improved mobility, improved balance and improved endurance. All things I think any athlete would want from their training, but for me this is about giving me an improved ability to live my life. When I miss my visits to the centre my body knows about it, and then so does my mind. The two are intrinsically linked. If I am moving better and feeling physically better then my mind can better manage the difficulties that this disease gives me day to day.'

As I was formulating the plan to do all the Wainwrights I knew it was also the perfect opportunity to raise money for MS charities. I decided to fundraise for both the Samson Centre and the national Multiple Sclerosis Society. I realised that if it went well I could raise a considerable amount. The downside of this was that it could not be a low-key attempt. I run not for fame or fortune and not for the publicity, but because I enjoy it and I love to challenge myself. Ideally I would like to go out and run the Wainwrights with just a few friends for support, but this was not going to be the case here. The more publicity I could create the more money I would raise. I would have to accept this and try to enjoy the publicity, but I knew there would be an increase in stress and worry as a result.

14   A LOGISTICAL MOUNTAIN TO CLIMB

Once I had decided to go for an attempt at all the Wainwright fells I had the whole autumn, winter and spring to come up with a good route, run over and reccie as much of it as possible, and train hard. I knew preparation would be the key to completing the Wainwrights. I needed to follow the meticulous preparations of Mark Seddon at the OMM and Mark Hartell and Mark McDermott on the Lake District twenty-four-hour record. These are great athletes but not the ultimate speed merchants. They know the importance of pacing, a great support crew, perfect knowledge of a route, and eating and drinking the right things. They try to leave absolutely nothing to chance.

The first thing on my extensive task list was to choose a good route. Joss Naylor and Alan Heaton, together with some friends, such as Ken Ledward, with an intimate knowledge of the fells, had obviously been through this process before, and I could have just looked at their routes and tweaked them a bit. But I didn't want to do this. If there was a better route, then using their routes as a starting point might mean I would miss a completely different and better route. So I started with a clean slate and an open mind about the best route. I plotted 214 dots on a map and started to think of different combinations of linking them all up. For those like me with a mathematical background it is a bit like the 'travelling salesman' problem of linking up destinations in the shortest possible route. However, as well as minimising distance I also needed to minimise the ascent and also find routes where the running was easier.

Unfortunately a computer program to pick the optimum route was probably impossible; it was back to the human mind and local knowledge. Some of the fells linked together neatly, but other fells were just impossible to join up in a satisfactory route. Binsey stands at the northern end of Bassenthwaite Lake. I just couldn't decide if it was better to include it as an 'out and back' during a loop of the northern fells, or between the northern fells and the north-western fells. Castle Crag in Borrowdale was another headache. This is the smallest Wainwright, so I would need a big descent on the way to it and then a big climb back up after visiting it. But from which other fells? I just couldn't find a good way of linking it up.

Eventually I *thought* I had a good route, so I plotted it up on the computer using Memory Map which gave me the distance and ascent. Having done this I then looked at Joss's route. Some of it – such as in the far eastern fells – was very similar, but other sections were very different. So his first and last fells were Whinlatter and Barrow and mine were Latrigg and Cat Bells. There were a couple of sections where Joss's route seemed a bit better so I decided to modify my route. I then asked my older sister Karen, and her husband, Dan, to see if they could come up with a better route, or whether they thought mine was spot on. The route they came up with was completely different from both Joss's and mine. As a result, I once again tweaked my route. Happily I thought I now finally had the *perfect* route.

However, it then occurred to me to look at it from a logistics viewpoint. I realised my route was totally crazy. There was a twenty-four-hour section, picking up thirty Wainwrights on both sides of the Ennerdale valley without any road crossings, and therefore without any access to the support vehicle. I had to change this section, which then affected everything else and so I had to re-plan the whole route. Finally, by April, I had settled on a good route with good logistics. I was happy that all the rockiest and roughest sections were completed by the end of the second day when I would be strongest and most able to cope with them, particularly if the weather was bad. I had spent over fifty hours looking over the maps and plotting different routes.

My final route gave a total flat distance of 519 kilometres (322 miles) with a total ascent of 35,000 metres, and daily values of eighty kilometres with 5,400 metres of ascent. This equated to nearly two marathons and four times up and down Ben Nevis each day. Although the two marathons a day seems a long way that was actually the easy bit. I can probably run two flat marathons on a road in seven hours, although I would hate every minute as it would be so boring. Much harder was the amount of ascent each day. Climbing at ten metres a minute, which is a reasonable speed, this would take nine hours – and then I'd also have to descend the same again.

I measured Joss's route on the computer using the same mapping software to check that mine was better and by how much. Joss's total distance was 535 kilometres with 37,000 metres of ascent, so I reckoned I had saved sixteen kilometres and 2,000 metres of ascent (around four per cent), which corresponded to around a four- to six-hour difference at the end of the attempt. I was delighted that all the hours I had spent looking at maps and planning a great route had made a substantial improvement.

As well as a better route, I also wanted to spend less time not moving than Joss. On his first three nights Joss stopped, was driven somewhere to have a nice meal, a sleep in the back of a van for around four hours, driven back to where he stopped and then started again – around seven to eight hours after stopping. My plan was that I should really only be either sleeping or moving; I should be trying to eat as much as possible while moving. So Joss's total time was 169 hours, of which he spent forty-four hours resting and 125 hours moving. I planned a total time of 158 hours with twenty-five hours resting and 133 hours moving. This meant that although I expected to be moving slower than Joss, I hoped to beat his time. It was a great plan but a lot harder to put into practice than to write down. I knew it would rely on really good support and me coping with no more than four hours of sleep each night.

So the support team was going to be really important. But, in fact, I needed two great support teams. Firstly, a support team who would look after me at the road crossings, sort out and wash my kit, feed me and have everything packed for a quick departure. Secondly, a fell support team: two or more people with me on every section of the run who would carry all my clothes, food and drink that I needed for that section, and a map with my planned route, as well as knowing which fell to go to next. These people needed to know when and where to meet and be provided with a rucksack containing all these essentials. What was crucial was having a single person in charge of all of this, someone who knew exactly where everyone should be at any time and had everything prepared for my arrival at each support point. This was going to be a week of driving round the Lake District with little sleep and continuous stress and hassle. It's the sort of job that you don't notice if it is done right, but if there is a mistake it can spell disaster.

In December, six months before my planned start, I went to Jane Saul's fiftieth birthday party in Hexham. I had known Jane from when we were both in the Northumberland Fell Runners and lived close to each other. She had been in charge of sorting everything out on my Lake District twenty-four-hour record attempts. Jane works as a contract manager for Arup engineering consultants, so she is good at sorting out both people and logistics. I asked her if she was keen to take on this job and, luckily for me, she said yes.

Jane: 'Steve sold it to me as a nice drive around the Lake District, meals in pubs and cafes, catch ups with Lakes mates … I just needed to be at support points with a bit of food and a bed for Steve. Little did I know how hard it was going to be! The first step was to work out where Steve was actually going. The route was very detailed, but drat, still in Steve's head.

Great for Steve, one of the best route planners and navigators about, but a bit hard for the rest of us mere mortals to work out where the route went and where Steve would be. So, my work colleague and fell runner, Andrew Higgins, had the privilege of being the first appointment to the support crew. Andrew and Steve plotted the route and all its many revisions on a digital Harvey's map of the Lake District. So then, phew, we had a route map and maps of each leg. But heck, Steve was going to run all over the Lakes in a very, very long, wiggly line … The enormity of it started to sink in.'

My next big job was getting financial support for my adventure. I was planning on leaving as little as possible to chance. This meant there would be quite a considerable amount of expenditure: two campervans for a week, petrol, parking, camping fees, food and drink, medical kit, clothes, shoes, mobile-phone bills. It all adds up. Before the Dragon's Back Race I had become a Berghaus athlete, so I went along with Jane to see them about some financial support. They were very happy to support my adventure, although they obviously wanted publicity in return, but they could immediately see the potential of my run from a marketing viewpoint and how the local media would happily run stories beforehand and afterwards. I find the media side of things very hard and I felt this would cause me another increase in pressure as a result of all the interviews I would have to give, but I just had to accept it. On the positive side, it would increase the awareness of my run and so would massively increase the potential to raise money for my MS charities.

Jane was very keen on me getting my fell support team sorted out. With twenty-four sections and two people on each section that's forty-eight people. Some people would do more than one section, so I was looking at around forty people. I wondered if I would be able to get this number of people – I hoped so as from many years of running fell races I am friends with a lot of people, but it was still a big ask. I decided the way to do it was to put a shout-out on social media and see who came forward to offer help. I wrote a post for sending out on Facebook, but sending the post was a massive decision. I knew what would happen as soon as I sent it: there would be loads of interest and amongst the fell-running community it would go viral. This was going to be a great way to get support but meant that suddenly my plan would be public knowledge. It would be extremely hard to back down. So I sat there for ten minutes wondering whether to press the send button. Eventually I did it. As expected, there was a massive interest and loads of offers of support. This was a great first step and although I needed to sort out which sections people could actually take on, it gave me the confidence that I would have enough people to come along and help me.

> Jane: 'The 'helping' task grew and grew, support runners and crew were required, there was a running schedule to be drafted, campervans needed to be hired, the support points all needed to be visited and checked, how to get runners back to their cars needed to be sorted, what food Steve would eat on the hill and at the support points had to be decided, what would the medical requirements be, how to get massages and physiotherapy for Steve, how to take photos on the hill and at the support points and get them on the blog, what kit would be needed, how to deal with washing? A list of Wainwrights in the right order was also needed. Nic Davies and Jon Bardgett were called upon to hold my hand, calm me down, ply me with coffee and divulge their many years of experience. My 'to do' list grew and grew, I also made a 'to do' list specially for Steve and, on occasion, refused to leave his house until some of them were done!'

I had worked out a route, but Jane sensibly kept on asking me about an actual schedule. She needed to know exactly when and where to meet me at the end of each of the twenty-four sections and who would be supporting me on each section. I was not keen on setting a schedule, not because I didn't think it was a good idea, but because I had no idea how fast I would be moving. However, I realised I had to create one, so I set to work with the aim of producing expected times for each peak and each support point on a spreadsheet. But what speed would I be going at? On the first day I set the speed to twenty-hour Bob Graham Round pace. Then after that I gradually reduced the speeds so that my final scheduled time was six days and fourteen hours. The times for each peak incorporated a flat speed and a climbing speed (plus a slight reduction in speed for the descent which I didn't bother changing as the week progressed), the main weakness being that it did not take into account the type of terrain (is it rocky, grassy or a good track?). On day one in the schedule my flat speed was twelve kilometres per hour and I was climbing at fifteen metres per minute. By day seven this was set to seven kilometres per hour flat speed and climbing at eight metres per minute.

Yet another facet I had to consider was publicity. Early on I decided two things were important regarding building and maintaining publicity: a regularly updated blog, and live tracking of my position. I thought these would keep people interested in my progress over the week. Little did I realise how important and popular these would become. The blog I updated every two weeks or so in the months leading up to my attempt. They took a while to write but it was great for me to record my thoughts. I obviously couldn't update the blog during the event but luckily Shane Ohly offered to do this for me, together with regular tweets of my progress … once I had sorted out registering with Twitter. For the tracker I contacted James Thurlow at Open Tracking.[1] He had provided me with a tracker for my Lake District twenty-four-hour record attempt and was happy to provide me with two trackers for the week – one to have with me and one as backup. The trackers weigh sixty-five grams and are a bit bigger than a matchbox. They work out their location using GPS and transmit this location every minute using mobile-phone technology,

---

1. *www.opentracking.co.uk*

selecting the best coverage available at every location. If no coverage is available all the locations and times are stored until reception becomes available. The trackers do have 'black spots' in the Lake District where they struggle to find any network coverage, particularly in some of the valleys such as Wasdale.

The latest position of the tracker would be displayed on an Ordnance Survey map on the Open Tracking website and this would update automatically. The overall route is also shown on the map together with the split times for each section.[2] This was perfect, as it would mean that anybody – including my support team – could see exactly where I was at any particular time and how I was doing against my schedule.

Jane: 'Steve was so laid back, any of my 'have you got the runners sorted?', was met with, 'yeah, there will be plenty, don't worry, they will just turn up'. But did they know where and when to turn up, or even in which week Steve was running? So 'the schedule' was born. Any supporters' names were added and the evolving gaps were sent back to Steve to get filled. I also organised the road-crossing support crew – mainly my mates (Alison Herberts, Elaine Cowie, Charles Scott and Dr Alison Scott). I invited them round for dinner and left the maps about. I might have sold it to them as pub stops, cafes, a week in the Lakes – that kind of thing. Again, little did they know! A good sense of humour was an essential prerequisite, as was an aversion to sleep, midge resistance, ability to drive campervans at any hour of the day or night, food preparation for Steve and runners, bottle washing, dish washing, an ability to source water, charm and sweet-talk whoever, photographing, cameraman, navigator, interviewer, cleaner, fetching and returning runners to cars, and bucket emptying – a very multi-talented bunch. Any mates living anywhere along the route were also roped in for checkpoint duty, food delivery and showers.'

2. www.steveb.opentracking.co.uk

15   PHYSICAL PREPARATION

I chatted to Joss Naylor a couple of times before I set out on this adventure. He said that the important thing is having run long distances on the fells for many years. He is of course right; to succeed you need to have the ability to move fast and yet be relaxed on the fells through rocks, heather, bracken and tussocks, both climbing and descending, and the only way to obtain this ability comes from many hours' running on the fells. Put a fast road runner on the fells and they would be able to run fast uphill on a good track but on the rest of any fell run they would really struggle. I am lucky in that I have been running through rough terrain with plenty of climbs and descents since I started orienteering when I was seven. I am also very relaxed when I am running on the fells, in fact so relaxed that when I fall over, which is regularly – I have something of a reputation for it – I almost always just roll and get straight back up without having hurt myself or lost much time. Living in the Lake District running every day on the fells has improved me further still. In particular I find the big, long descents much easier. I am much less tired than I used to be at the bottom of these descents and so faster on the next climb.

As well as having a background of running on the fells, it was also important to get a solid winter of training in. So while I was trying to sort out my route and all the other preparations needed, working, and trying to spend some time with my family, I was also training hard. It was a very difficult balancing act. I am lucky that, although I work for Newcastle University, I work from home on most days and I only need to go to Newcastle one day a week. That is a long day, as it's a two-and-a-half-hour commute each way, so I don't usually get a run in that day. I am also contracted to only work three days a week, although as I want to do a good job and I am aware that it is a privilege to be allowed to work at home, it tends to be four days a week spread out over five days.

Training for fell running where I live is usually a pleasure. Normally I get changed into my running clothes and walk to the barn where there is a covered area, open on two sides. Here I have a pile of fifteen pairs of shoes suitable for different sorts of terrain: trail, rock, mud and ice. They are in different states of repair from nearly new, which I save for racing, to those that are on their 'last legs' which are just about ready to throw away. I never wash my shoes as they will be muddy within five minutes of starting my next run, so after I finish running I take them off, put them in the big pile and let them dry naturally, which might take several days but I always have another dry pair to select. The best thing about this is my smelly running shoes never enter the house, which Emma really appreciates. Having selected my shoes I think about how I am feeling and what the weather is like. In my mind I decide on my route and just start running. If it's a nice sunny day and if I have time I will climb to the top of one of the fells, often Blencathra; if it is wet and windy I will usually take a lower level or valley route. The route to Blencathra takes me across fields down to the river and back up across more fields to the major A66 road, which I reach after about fifteen minutes of running. After this the 650-metre climb up Blencathra starts. The fastest route to the top is up Doddick Fell, one of five ridges leading down off the south side of Blencathra, which takes around thirty minutes from the road. I know I am going well when I find it easy to run all the way to the top. The descent back to the road takes me thirteen minutes at top speed, but that is hard on the legs and normally I jog down in under twenty minutes. Then it is back home across the fields and the end of a very enjoyable eighty-minute (or so) run.

The times when running is not a pleasure are when I am doing a hill interval or fartlek session. These sessions are designed to be painful and they are. However, I always enjoy that brilliant feeling when I have finished when the stress and hassles of work are gone and I feel happy and relaxed. I equate these sessions to an inverse hangover. In the hangover there is a long period of suffering after a short, enjoyable and happy period of drinking. In an interval session there is a long period of enjoyment and happiness after a short period of suffering.

Running for me is really therapeutic. When I am doing some computer coding and it's not working my frustration builds and builds. I can get very annoyed. If I am by myself at home I can even start shouting and swearing at the computer. Eventually I will go out for a run. After about twenty minutes my body will relax and my mind will wander into an almost dreamlike state. Suddenly I will work out how to fix the problem, often when I am not even thinking about it. Somehow going away from the problem and letting my mind relax allows it to find the solution. Although I have improved considerably I still tend to worry about the small things, and can become stressed before doing a talk in front of people, for example. Sometimes I might have a drink or two before such a talk, but actually a hard run is equally effective at stopping me worrying and has none of the negative side effects of drinking.

As long as I stay warm I enjoy training in the rain and wind in winter as much as on a warm summer day. Berghaus have some brilliant lightweight warm and waterproof kit so my core is generally fine; my problem is my hands. Even when I am wearing gloves, they can get very sore in cold, wet and windy weather, and the older I get the worse they seem to be. If you ever see me standing somewhere circling my arms round and round it will be because I am trying to get the circulation going and some warm blood into my hands. Another weakness I have is not making myself get up early to run before any of the rest of the family wakes up. It would be good if I could do it regularly, as it is a great way to start the day, and when I do manage it I feel great for the rest of the day. But I rarely seem to be able to do it. I really need a good eight hours' sleep a night and when I do eventually manage to crawl out of bed, my mind doesn't work properly for the first half hour. I cannot hold a conversation and even making breakfast is hard. So, I do most of my runs late in the morning or early in the afternoon. I also enjoy running in the evening but I need to be very careful with when and how much I eat or I will get my sore bowel problem.

The following was a typical week during the winter before my attempt:

Monday: 50 minutes easy
Tuesday: 1 hour 30 minutes hard
Wednesday: work in Newcastle
Thursday: 50 minutes including hill intervals or fartlek
Friday: 1 hour easy
Saturday: 2 hours easy
Sunday: 3–4 hours easy

This was around ten hours a week of running with around 4,000 metres of climbing. It was a mixture of easy and fast but I do tend to always run hard on the big steep climbs (to keep on running up these climbs is actually *hard*). I don't count distance, or even have a training diary, as it doesn't seem relevant on the fells. This typical week is probably around 80 to 100 kilometres, whereas on a flat road I would be doing nearer to 160 kilometres in ten hours. Every month or so I also fitted in a long (eight hours or so) run, although with an easier week beforehand. I tend to listen to my body and from experience I know if I am doing too much training and racing. This happened in 2001 when I was doing a mixture of fell racing, adventure racing and mountain marathons. Over the summer I competed every weekend in a long race. I was fit and running well. However, I started to struggle; it was not very obvious at first but people who would usually be just behind me in a fell race were just in front. But it got gradually worse; I was working really hard but getting poorer results. In adventure races and mountain marathons my team or partner started carrying a lot more of the weight so I could just about keep up. Finally my body decided it had had enough, I had overdone it. It got to the stage where I could not even run a mile and I had to get the lift up three floors to my office at work. My resting pulse was ten beats per minute above normal but when I went to the doctor for a blood test they found nothing wrong. I personally think it was some sort of virus but it was impossible to know. What I do know is that it took three months to recover and another three to build up my training and get fit again.

The weekdays at home are normally really busy, with both of us working, taking the children to and from the school bus and various after-school clubs. So it is important not to waste any time and this meant that in the winter before my attempt all my runs during the week were from my house. However, at the weekend I drove further afield and reccied sections of the route. It was good fun going up some different fells trying to find new and faster lines. There was one exceptionally horrible day when I reccied a section on the fells south of Ullswater. It was so windy that for ten minutes I tried to run along a section into the wind but I failed to make any progress, I would move forward a few metres then I would be pushed back a few metres. Not only could I not move forward, I couldn't see anything either with the horizontal rain blowing into my eyes – I really needed snow goggles. I started to become a bit worried but eventually I managed to crawl down off the fell, back to the car and drive home before all the roads flooded.

Over the spring and early summer I reduced my training time but increased the intensity with both an interval session and hill reps every week. On the spring bank holiday weekend at the end of May, three weeks before the start of my Wainwrights run, I had a final, really hard weekend of training. On the Saturday I did an eight-hour run on the fells followed by a two-and-a-half-hour fell race on the Sunday, and another eight-hour run on the fells on the Monday. The next weekend I did the thirty-two-kilometre Duddon Valley fell race. It is a great race but I felt shattered from the start. There was just nothing in my legs. It was time to recover in the final two weeks. However, a complete rest just does not work for me. I just stiffen up and find it really hard and painful to start running again. I also seem to struggle with my breathing if I have not exerted myself recently. So I had some rest days but I also went out three times in both the final two weeks, running between eight and ten kilometres each time at a steady pace. It stopped me stiffening up but was easy enough for me to recover and get my strength back.

I have always tried to eat healthily, with lots of fruit and vegetables and little processed food, so I did not make any changes to my diet. I thought about trying to lose three kilograms to get to my racing weight of seventy-three kilograms (eleven stone seven pounds) from my normal weight of seventy-six kilograms (twelve stone). In fell races these three kilograms seem to make a big difference, but this was different. Speed was not an issue; keeping a steady pace for up to seven days was all that mattered. I knew I would never be able to eat as many calories as I was burning and there would probably be times when I would be feeling really sick and unable to eat, so having a small amount of extra in reserve might actually help. So I made the decision not to try and lose any weight. I also made sure some of my long runs were done without any food so my body adapted to using its fat stores.

As well as being fit I also needed to make sure I had no injuries or even any niggles that would get worse over the week and cause a premature end to my run. At the start of the year I was still getting nerve pains down my leg if I landed awkwardly. So over the winter and spring I had some sort of treatment every week. This was either physiotherapy, acupuncture or sports massage. I also did some self-treatment by putting a hockey ball or a potato underneath particularly tight points in my legs and then applying my weight to it. I have never been good at stretching but for this I did set aside some time for regular sessions. The combination of all this seemed to work and the niggles gradually disappeared. But all the treatments and stretching were more time commitments when I did not really have any more time.

16   MAKING A MOVIE

I first met Alastair Lee at a Berghaus athlete weekend in January 2014. He had recently returned from Antarctica where he had been filming Leo Houlding, Jason Pickles and the rest of the team on their successful attempt at climbing Ulvetanna. During the day we had a discussion about kit. As usual I was mostly very quiet and did not get involved in many of the discussions. That evening we had a meal in Durham and then went out and had lots to drink in the local pubs. Eventually we ended up in a night-club. I am not much of a fan of nightclubs but once I was there I got into it.

> **Al Lee:** *'Steve is the archetypal English gentleman, a very gentle giant. I first met Steve in the reception of a hotel in Durham for a Berghaus athlete weekend. I was sat with Jason and Leo having a pint when Steve came over and introduced himself, pleasantries were exchanged and my immediate impression was that he's a pleasant guy to be around. The next day we had a long discussion about kit and then a social evening in Durham. As the evening wore on we went to a nightclub. The place was full of students, generally inebriated, and the music was of the super-high tempo, post-acid-house kind that is hard to take seriously. The students loved it, the stage was packed and the whistles and glow sticks were just about holding the insane rhythm. The number of athletes had dwindled and typically for a get together the last men standing were Leo, Jason and I, enjoying ourselves and having a laugh. Jason came over with another round of drinks and who should he point out bouncing along with the beat? It was only our mild-mannered fell-running acquaintance*

clearing the crowd as he bounced around the platform grinning amongst the glow sticks and almost taking out the stage lights. Jason and I looked at each other confirming 'Steve is a top guy, brilliant'.

'A couple of weeks later having friended Steve on Facebook I came across his YouTube video that explained his Wainwrights run.[1] The video was around five minutes long and in this time a blue graphic line would travel up and down all the Lakeland fells as Steve casually described how many peaks he would climb each day and roughly how far he would travel and for how long each day. I was utterly gobsmacked at this proposed feat, knowing those fells as I do and knowing the effort it takes to climb one or two of the big ones and yet here was Steve claiming he would climb thirty a day for seven consecutive days. Insane! I'd never really been interested in fell running or thought of making a film about the subject but having got to know Steve a little bit and seeing this proposed feat of endurance I just had to get involved.'

Alastair makes superb climbing and mountaineering films and he also has a book of amazing Lake District photographs. So I knew if he made a film it would be good. However, I also thought it would add another layer of stress knowing that I was being filmed a lot of the time, so to start with I wasn't entirely sure about it. But, I talked to him some more and he was really reassuring and told me that he would try really hard not to get in the way and, whether I succeeded or failed, as long as he could capture the emotions of my journey through the fells he would be happy. I also knew that the publicity would help in my fundraising attempts and afterwards I would have a film about me made by a professional film-maker, which hopefully I could look back at happily in years to come. So I decided to take up Al on his offer.

Before the attempt I spent three days out filming with Al. Each time this involved going from Threlkeld up Hall's Fell to the summit of Blencathra.

1. *www.youtube.com/watch?v=tlowtyx9cME*

This was a great location as it is a rocky ridge with easy access and amazing views. One time we carried several big tubes of metal up to make a boom but it was too windy to use. On another occasion we took a drone (Hexacopter) up and the weather was perfect so we got some great images looking down on me running along the ridge.

Al had never done a running film and as it is so different from a climbing film he knew it was going to be difficult. On a climbing film you can often go back to a location and get another take whereas this is impossible when running. I was definitely not going to go back and climb a mountain again! So his plan was to come out every day and capture the high-quality shots with his expensive, heavy cameras but also to have my support team filming with a couple of handy-cams. He gave a list of instructions to my support team, with one being that if I threatened to hit them then that was the moment to press record!

17　TWO-WEEK COUNTDOWN

Emma wrote in my blog:

'Only a couple of weeks to go, and I think Steve has realised how much organising this is going to take. He's quite happy with the running bit; it's the logistics that he leaves to the last minute. Jane came round yesterday and did her best to sort him out.

Jane: 'Have you got someone to help on each leg?'
Steve: 'I think most of them.'
Jane: 'Do they know which leg they are doing?'
Steve: 'Probably not.'
Jane: 'Do you think you should tell them?
Steve: 'OK I'll try.'

I don't know what we would do without Jane. Steve now has a 'to do' list which I think he is working through. Yesterday, he asked my advice on setting up a Twitter account, which is a good start, although not very help-ful as I am hardly an expert. I have to somehow work out what food he needs to take, where and when I can meet him (bearing in mind I will be looking after three children who won't appreciate being dragged out of bed at 3 a.m.), how I am going to wash twenty-four sets of smelly running gear, how I will manage all this around getting the children to school, going to work (I work five days a week for the Lake District National Park, I can take some days' leave, but not the full week), helping out at James's school residential, looking after various people who may or may not be staying with us and trying to coordinate who has to be where when. Meanwhile the house is descending into complete chaos, Hannah says she would like to live in a new house "without dirty bits in it". Hmm, maybe it's time to stop writing and get on with some other stuff ... '

I could feel the pressure was beginning to grow and I wrote the following in my blog:

'June 14th has been etched on my mind for a long time but it now seems to be really close. I have really mixed feelings about the whole thing. At times I feel really excited about doing it and cannot wait to start. I think of all the other races and training I have done and I think I have a really good chance of breaking the record. Then suddenly my feelings change completely and I am daunted and scared by the length of the route and keeping going for twenty hours a day. I feel the pressure of having forty or so people out to support me (thanks everyone for the help) having taken time off work and away from their families. I worry that it will all go wrong and I will get an injury early on and have to pull out. Then I think that everyone is happy to help and they will understand completely if I do have to pull out.'

As well as the pressure of having a large support team, there were other strains. There were the media interviews. In the last two weeks leading up to the run there were two filming sessions with local television channels, four interviews for outdoor magazines, the filming by Al Lee, and I was also trying to do lots of social media posts and my blog so I could raise more money for the MS charities. It all seemed so different from the simplicity of just going out and running.

I received regular packages from Berghaus containing all the kit I would need for the week. This included: fifteen base-layer tops, ten warmer tops, six waterproofs (of various weights), twenty-four pairs of socks, leggings, hats, gloves, sleeping bags, rucksacks, walking poles and trail shoes. Overall I had ten pairs of shoes of different sizes and for different terrain. Jane took the final week leading up to the run off work. She picked up the campervan we were hiring from my teammate in Borrowdale Fell Runners, Paul 'Corny' Cornforth, and the second one we were hiring, an old VW camper, from Keswick. She sorted food for the week, all my clothes and maps of every section. She was also making loads of changes to the schedule as my support team was in a constant state of flux due to births, deaths (not the runners), work shift changes, injuries and illness.

3 Taking on the Wainwrights

Overleaf: The start of my Wainwrights round outside Keswick Moot Hall with my family. **Photo:** Steve Birkinshaw Collection.

Forcing down a pot of rice pudding on the climb up Glaramara with Jim Mann. **Photo:** Steve Birkinshaw Collection.

18   DAY ONE

SECTION 1   Keswick to Borrowdale School
DETAIL   31.9km, 1,730m ascent, 11 Wainwrights
SUPPORT TEAM   Paul 'Corny' Cornforth and Nic Barber
TIMES   Start time 09.00, end time 13.50, break at end of leg 00.09

So the big day has arrived. I am desperate to get going but I am also desperately trying to stay calm and relaxed so as not to waste any energy. I have done everything I can to be perfectly prepared for this run. The training has gone well, the logistics and support are sorted enough for me to forget about them and leave to Jane to sort out. Amazingly the weather for the week looks dry and warm. The weather is often the key to an attempt such as this and is obviously outside my control. If it is too hot, like during Joss's attempt, then it can be really hard work with dehydration and heat stroke a big problem. On the other hand, wet and windy weather makes the rocks slippery, navigation difficult and there is the inverse problem of hypothermia. Overall, I am delighted to have settled, dry and warm weather – which also makes it so much easier and more enjoyable for the support team. The first day looks slightly too hot and very humid, but if I can cope with this then the rest of the week looks great. I decided on a 9 a.m. start so I can get a decent night's sleep before I begin and so I'm not sleep deprived on the first day. Despite my nerves I slept well; it helps sleeping in my own bed.

After a quick breakfast Jane drives me to Keswick. We get there at 8.30 a.m. and there are lots of market traders setting up their stalls but no one else around. A few people gradually appear including my support team on this section, Corny and Nic. Corny lives locally and is self-employed while Nic is having a break from work before he starts a PhD so both say they will come out and support me quite a lot over the week. James Thurlow also turns up with the trackers.

My family turn up with around five minutes to go. I hug them, pose for a few photos and climb the steps to the Moot Hall, feeling quite scared waiting for the clock to strike 9 a.m. I am scared of the pain I expect to push myself through over the next seven days. The accounts of the pain that Alan and Joss went through are clear in my mind.

The clock strikes and I set off. Nic and Corny join me and we are running towards Latrigg and the first of the 214 Wainwrights. Nic and Corny have a rucksack each with my spare clothes, food and drink for the section and the tracker. I relax and I am happy to forget all the logistics and media side of things and do what I do best and enjoy, which is running on the fells.

It is already hot as we begin the steep climb to the summit of Latrigg, so I take my shirt off. Then as we reach the top I look around at the view and twist my ankle. It's OK this time, but I need to be more careful. I am deliberately walking up the hills and running steadily on the descents and flats. It is hard to know what speed to go at but I am happy as long as it is a relaxed and comfortable pace. Nic has all my split times with him and it is interesting to compare my speed with these. On the climbs I am picking up time, on the flat about the same but downhill I am losing time. But it depends on how rough the terrain is, as that was not factored into my calculation. On a rough descent I am losing quite a lot of time.

It is fast-going on the first five tops and we pick up quite a lot of time, but then we turn off the paths on to the tussocks and heather. When it is fairly flat I struggle to work out if I should be running or walking over this terrain. I can easily manage to run but I want to conserve my energy. However, whether I run or walk it is hard work with both a high temperature and a high humidity, and I am sweating excessively. This combination of heat and humidity is my least favourite weather condition; I think because I am quite big, I produce a lot of heat and sweat a lot. The guys do a great job giving me food and drink but I am finding the conditions really sapping. I am mainly eating Torq bars and drinking a mixture of Torq energy drink and water.

> **Corny:** *'As we approach Castle Crag, the last top on this section, Steve turns to me and says he is feeling really tired and asks me if I am feeling tired. I am feeling really tired having been running hard and carrying his spare kit, food and drink for the last four hours, but I say I am feeling OK. However, it is not looking good feeling tired after four hours with six and a half days to go.'*

We reach the River Derwent after descending from Castle Crag for the final flat mile of this section. Nic runs ahead to Borrowdale School to warn the support team of my arrival and let them know what food to have out. I try to suggest sensible food, but I don't really feel like anything. When we finally arrive it is great to see the support team including Emma, and also my children sitting on the top of our car. After I left

Keswick the support team rushed back to my house to finish packing the campervans for a week driving round the Lake District. So when I arrive at Borrowdale School I am brilliantly looked after. First I take off my shoes and socks, I have a wash (using a sponge together with a bucket of water), Emma rubs in some suncream for me and I put on fresh shorts. I then sit down on a deck chair with a massive range of food in front of me. I manage to force down a cheese sandwich, some crisps and tomatoes. I have a drink of tea and some water. Finally I get some dry socks on and choose my shoes for the next section. After nine minutes I am ready to go.

SECTION 2	Borrowdale School to Loweswater Village Hall
DETAIL	40km, 3,180m ascent, 19 Wainwrights
SUPPORT TEAM	Andrew 'Scoffer' Schofield, Jim Mann, Mark Roberts (first half) and Malcolm Patterson (second half)
TIMES	Start time 13.59, end time 22.17, break at end of leg 00.20

This is the longest section of the whole round and the one with the most climbing. Nearly marathon distance and with 3,180 metres of ascent, which is three and a half times the climb up from Wasdale Head to England's highest mountain, Scafell Pike. Not only that, but the first half is rough and rocky with a lot of it off the paths. I am planning on doing it in just over eight hours, so the speed has to be fast. However, as soon as I set off I feel tired and bloated. The heat and humidity are overpowering – I am sweating profusely but instead of it evaporating and cooling me down the sweat is just dripping off me. I have to walk the first ten minutes, thinking 'will I be able to pick up the speed?'

For this section I originally had only Scoffer helping me. Scoffer is the ideal person for this leg as he lives just near Borrowdale School and knows these fells as well as anyone, having run and raced over them for more than twenty years – I know I won't have to worry about which way to go as he knows all the fastest lines. Jim was planning to be away working in Israel but luckily for me there was a last-minute change of plan so he could jump in his car and drive two hours from north-east England and come and help me. Having Mark Roberts was even luckier for me but not for him. The previous day he was out with a hedge trimmer when he slipped and chopped through the top part of one of his fingers leaving it hanging on with just a bit of skin. After an operation he had it nicely taped up and he also had a week off work on sick leave. Although he couldn't work he could run without any problem, as long as he didn't fall on his damaged finger. This meant he could come out and run with me every day.

The climb up to Bessyboot from Rosthwaite Fell is one I know well from the Borrowdale Fell Race and I know I am struggling. I stagger up the steep rocky slope and as much as I want to I cannot eat the rice pudding the guys are carrying for me. Eventually as I climb up Glaramara, an hour after starting this section, I manage to force it down. Luckily for me the clouds are building up and soon after Glaramara the drizzle comes in. It is still very warm and I do not need to put my shirt back on, but the cooling effect of the rain directly on my skin is very dramatic and I quickly go from struggling to feeling good. As we drop off Allen Crags I avoid looking towards Esk Hause, knowing I will be passing within 500 metres of this point in thirty hours' time. I concentrate on the hills we are doing today.

As we approach Seathwaite Fell we have a discussion about which is the Wainwright, no one is quite sure; we know which the highest point is but think Wainwright might have selected the small top at the northern end of the ridge, which although slightly lower has a better view. The guys get their phones out and do a quick Google search and this confirms the Wainwright is the top at the northern end of the ridge. The descent from Seathwaite Fell is steep with lots of crags and it would be really frustrating to get crag-fast and lose some valuable minutes. However,

Scoffer has reccied the route so that we descend mostly on steep grass with some small bits of scree. We have an equally steep route back up the other side to Base Brown but have a nice surprise as Scoffer has stashed some Coke and Eccles cakes, which both go down well. With the cloud still around and light drizzle I am feeling strong over the highest summits of this section, including Great Gable, where we pass some people going the other way towards the end of a Bob Graham Round.

> Jim Mann: *'Steve had long periods of good form and was particularly strong on the hills going over Great Gable and Kirk Fell. Stopping to refill our water bottles it was a struggle to catch back up and I had to work hard; Steve was taking a no-nonsense approach, and running hard lines in the hills, pretty much straight lining everything, ignoring the easier running on the less direct paths and taking a real mountain marathon approach.'*

Eventually we reach the old tramway path above Honister Pass. Here we have a change of personnel with Malcolm taking over from Mark, and I can have a sit down for a couple of minutes. I feel tired and do not really feel like getting up again but I have a really long way to go and a schedule to keep to. Malcolm was a really good runner in the past so he and Scoffer reminisce about all the old fell races and racers. There is lots of discussion about the lack of strength of depth amongst the current crop of top fell racers, about times that would have put you in the top fifty in results twenty years ago putting you in the top ten these days. It is interesting, particularly as I am trying to break a twenty-eight-year-old record, and it takes my mind off the long days I have coming up. Soon we are heading towards Haystacks and I can see Al Lee and Rob Jarman are there ready to film us.

Al Lee: *'I knew producing a really good running film was going to be difficult, there would be none of the dramatic shots of a climbing film, just Steve's steady but relentless progress with top after top. There would also be no second chances to capture Steve as he ran past. The first place I decided to catch Steve was as he approached Haystacks. I hoped there would be some stunning footage of Innominate Tarn just behind Steve and the Western Fells in the distance, all in the beautiful evening light. It was very hot and humid (almost tropical) on the walk up to Haystacks with Rob Jarman, and hard work with packs of twenty kilograms. We got the shot perfectly set up but as Steve approached the summit he took a path I wasn't expecting which took him behind some rocks and so I didn't capture the footage I wanted. Then I had the wrong lens in the camera to film him when he was close by. It couldn't have been much worse. I was devastated that all that effort had gone to waste.'*

I feel a bit bad that we didn't go on the path that Al was expecting. Luckily he doesn't ask me to go back and do it again. I would have refused anyway, I have far enough to run without redoing bits. The ridge along past High Crag and High Stile between Ennerdale Water and Buttermere is beautiful – a mixture of rock and grass along an obvious path. The rain has now stopped and the clouds have lifted to give a wonderful evening. However, it is still hot and I have not put my shirt back on. I am making reasonable progress and just about keeping to the schedule, picking up a minute or two on the climbs and losing bits on the descents. However, we are running short of water so Jim offers to drop down and find a nice spring to fill our bottles. I am still regularly eating bars and getting them down OK but not really enjoying them.

Jane has arranged for the support point at the end of the section to be at Loweswater village hall, which is good news as there is plenty of flat space there for everyone to meet. We arrive thirteen minutes up on schedule, which is great, and without any injury problems or blisters –

it has been a good start. I have a quick wash outside but as it is just past
10 p.m. and still warm and humid, the midges are out. I have a thing
about midges – I really hate them. They seem to be drawn to me and
when they bite me I swell up and am really sore for about fifteen minutes,
although after that I'm fine. My tired state seems to be making me even
more sensitive to their bites. As I wash I get a midge bite on my foot,
which for me is the worst place, we rush into the campervan but it is too
late. For the next ten minutes I am nearly screaming in agony. Anyone
that comes into the campervan thinks the pain of thirteen hours of
running is too much for me, and are relieved to find out it is only midges.
My support crew realise how wimpy I am with midges and will try and
make sure I am outside as little as possible at the support points.

SECTION 3	Loweswater Village Hall to Ennerdale Water Car Park
DETAIL	17.1km, 920m ascent, 5 Wainwrights
SUPPORT TEAM	Andy Bradley, Nic Barber and Richard Suddaby
TIMES	Start time 22.37, end time 01.49, break at end of leg 03.15

I feel bloated and stiff as I descend from the campervan. I grab my poles
for the first time and walk off along the road with Andy, Nic and Richard.
Although it's turning dark I am in safe hands as Andy lives nearby and so
knows these fells very well. After about five minutes I begin to jog slowly
to the start of the first climb. The climb is very pleasant with the poles
getting my arms and back working as well as my legs. After a brief discussion it is obvious the top I have reccied is not the first Wainwright on this
section. The actual Wainwright is out and back along the ridge and not
the highest point. The run to the second Wainwright on this section is
pleasant, undulating and grassy. I try to eat a bar as we ascend the final
short climb to this summit, but it's not going down well. I am struggling
to swallow it, but after lots of chewing I eventually get it down. However, as we start descending my stomach goes from feeling bloated to

exceptionally uncomfortable. I feel sick, I tell the guys and hope it will go away. Suddenly I know I am going to be sick. There is nothing that can be done about it apart from to stop, kneel over and make sure I throw up on the grass and not on myself. One lot of sick comes up, I have a ten-second rest, then another lot. After the fourth my stomach is empty.

The guys look very worried and think this might be the end. I have thrown up four times before while out running, most recently at my Lake District twenty-four-hour record attempt, but also with forty kilometres to go at the Fellsman race in Yorkshire. From these exper-iences and races where I have felt really sick but never actually been sick I know it can sometimes be better to bring it up rather than just feeling terrible for hours and hours. I will be able to carry on and complete the section, albeit at a slower than normal pace, but I will need to recover and rest well at Ennerdale so I am OK for tomorrow. So we set off again, walking slowly to start with but after about five minutes picking up speed to a gentle jog. But how long will I last before I completely run out of energy? I spot a bottle of Lucozade Sport in Andy's rucksack. Despite the fact that he is really looking forward to it, he kindly lets me have it, and that keeps me going to the end of the section.

Meanwhile, a lot of the country's attention is focused on the rain-forests of Brazil as England are playing Italy at Manaus in the football world cup. Many people in England are very excited but all is quiet out on the fells. It is no surprise to find that Italy have won. The football players will go off for some rest and recovery for five days before their next match. However, it is a strange thought that during the same period of time I will get hardly any rest. For twenty hours a day I will be moving, climbing and descending, Wainwright after Wainwright. If all goes to plan, even when they have finished their second match I will still have twenty-four hours to go.

Eventually we reach Ennerdale Water and have an amazing run along the edge of the lake, which looks beautiful as the moon reflects off its smooth surface. It is great to see the campervans and I am looking forward to a well-earned rest. The first day is done. It was hard, harder than I thought and did not go as planned but I am still on schedule – thirty-one minutes up – and I have no injury problems. I had originally thought that I might just have a short stop here and then continue going. My support team have to be ready to go at a moment's notice if I decide to go for the short stop. However, after being sick I know I need a decent amount of time for my stomach to recover and get some energy back inside me, so I decide to go for a three-hour stop and hopefully a two-hour sleep. If I can recover I still have a chance of completing the Wainwrights. I have a quick wash, rush into the campervan to get away from the midges and over the next thirty minutes I manage to get down a Torq recovery drink and half a plate of food. I have been given the bigger, more comfortable campervan with Emma, while everyone else squeezes into the old VW van. We lie down and try to get some sleep.

Emma: *'After getting the kids to sleep at my mum and dad's house in Gosforth I head out to Ennerdale, in time to see a really rough-looking Steve jog in. His support team describe in detail how he has thrown up loads, and as that is what finished off his second attempt at the Lake District twenty-four-hour record I know it is bad news. However, unlike the twenty-four-hour record he does have a bit of time in hand, so it is not the end of his attempt, as long as he can keep some food down and get a good night's sleep. Although that is easier said than done. To start with he needs food, drink, and a change of clothes including his compression tights, none of which I can find in the camper van. It is the first time I have been in it and like most campervans it has lots of clever storage compartments, which are impossible to find, particularly when you can't even find the light switches. Jane has everything in hand, but is understandably shattered and desperate to get to sleep, but I have to keep bothering her. Eventually we get sorted and Steve tries but fails to get to sleep. He keeps getting up for wees and groaning about things hurting, he is pretty low psychologically, and it is hard to know what to say to make him feel better when I am not convinced myself that he can do this. At this point I would rate his chances of completing the whole round at around twenty per cent. It is one of those nights when you are glad it is time to get up as it takes away the misery of lying awake. I tell his support team he is in a bad way and they say not to worry, they will sort him out, and he hobbles off. Back at my mum and dad's house in Gosforth, I head straight for bed and I am just dropping off to sleep when Hannah's little voice in my ear says "It's morning now, let's get up!" so I have no choice but to go without sleep that night.'*

It is exceptionally frustrating lying here shattered but unable to sleep. I try to just accept that I am not tired enough and that just lying down resting is nearly as good as sleeping, but it's still hard. I think the caffeine is keeping me awake but as well as that my knees are throbbing. There is not any swelling, they just hurt, like someone is squeezing them really hard. However, I struggled similarly with sore knees at night on the Dragon's Back Race so I think they will be fine tomorrow once I get moving again.

01

Stephen Palmer (WCH) National M10 Champion, receives his prize from
Mr Denis Howell, MP, Minister for Sport.

02 03

01 Walking in the Brecon Beacons, aged eight, with my sister Karen, 1976. **Photo:** Steve Birkinshaw Collection.

02 Picture from the *National Orienteering* magazine after coming third in the ten-and-under class at the
British Orienteering Championships, 1977.

03 Local newspaper photo after winning the East Anglian Junior Orienteering Team competition in 1978 with
(L–R) Julian, me, Karen, Susan Braggins and Hilary. **Photo:** Steve Birkinshaw Collection.

04

05

06

04 Elite win with Mark Seddon at the Karrimor International Mountain Marathon (KIMM) in the Howgills (known as the Howling Howgills that year due to the extreme wind and rain), 1998. **Photo:** Steve Birkinshaw Collection.

05 Trophies for winning the 2009 Lake District Mountain Trial in Eskdale, Lake District. **Photo:** Steve Birkinshaw Collection.

06 Crossing the finish line to win the 2012 Berghaus Dragon's Back Race. **Photo:** Rob Howard.

07 Climbing towards Loft Crag on day three of the Wainwrights. **Photo:** Steve Ashworth.

08 Descending from Pike of Stickle with Ben Turner on day three of the Wainwrights. **Photo:** Steve Ashworth.

Map overleaf Lake District Ordnance Survey 1:250,000-scale map showing the route.

07

08

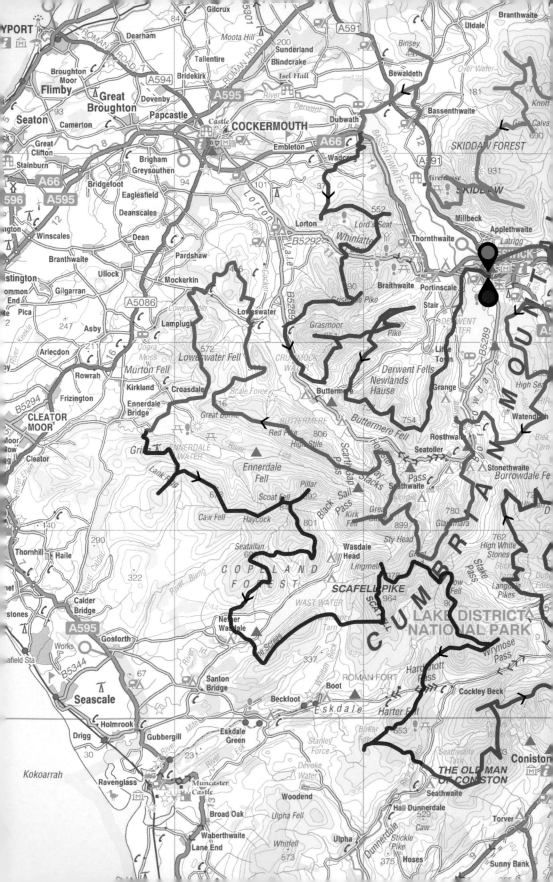

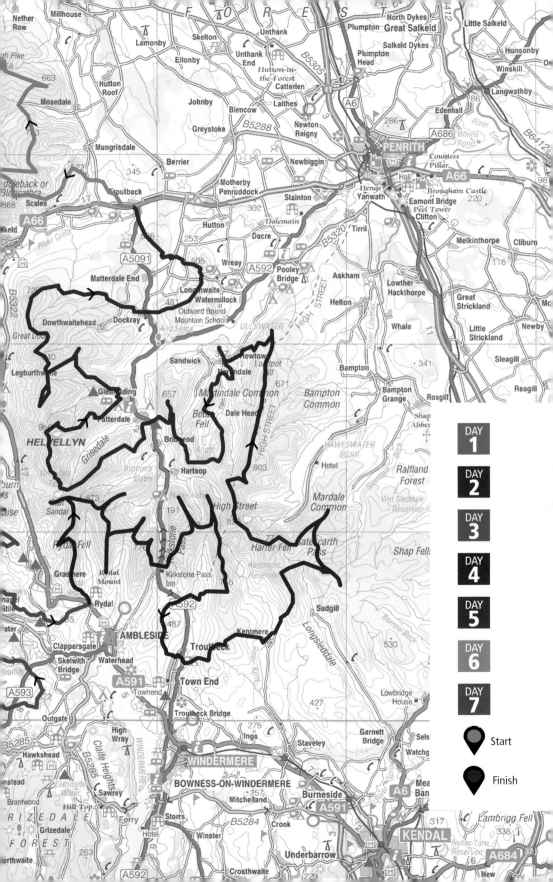

DAY
1

DAY
2

DAY
3

DAY
4

DAY
5

DAY
6

DAY
7

Start

Finish

09 Climbing to the summit of Pike of Stickle with David Armstrong on day three of the Wainwrights. **Photo:** Steve Ashworth.

10 Gavin Bland and Andrew Davies bursting one of my blisters on Mardale Ill Bell on day four of the Wainwrights.
Photo: Steve Birkinshaw Collection.

11 Emma helps with my asthma inhaler on day five of the Wainwrights. **Photo:** Steve Birkinshaw Collection.

12 Contouring back round below the summit of Skiddaw on day six of the Wainwrights. **Photo:** Steve Birkinshaw Collection.

13 In extreme pain with Mel Culleton-Wright sorting out my feet while Phil Davies gives me a massage.
Mosedale Road End on day six of the Wainwrights. **Photo:** Steve Birkinshaw Collection.

14 Having a five-minute powernap on the summit of Great Cockup on day six of the Wainwrights. **Photo:** Paul Dobson.

12

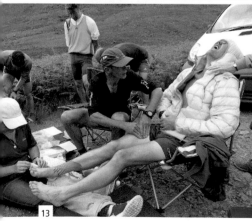

13

14

15   Taking the pressure off my blisters by bum shuffling down toward the Hobcarton car park. **Photo:** Mike Pearson.

16   Climbing up Rannerdale Knotts with Lewis Taylor and Vicky Ware on day seven of the Wainwrights, using my normal technique of hands as well as feet as it is very steep. **Photo:** Steve Birkinshaw Collection.

17   The final run up to the Moot Hall to complete my Wainwrights round. **Photo:** Steve Birkinshaw Collection.

18   The finish of my Wainwrights round with my family on the steps of the Moot Hall, Keswick. **Photo:** Paul Dobson.

Everything prepared by the support team for my arrival at the Wasdale Rare Goats Farm Yard. **Photo:** Steve Birkinshaw Collection.

19 DAY TWO

SECTION 4   Ennerdale Water Car Park to Wasdale Rare Goats Farm Yard

DETAIL   32.4km, 2,450m ascent, 13 Wainwrights

SUPPORT TEAM   Andy Bradley, Bill Williamson, Richard McGrath
and Tom Brunt

TIMES   Start time 05.04, end time 12.16, break at end of leg 00.20

My support team are woken up and told I will be ready to go in thirty minutes, once I have eaten my breakfast porridge and banana. However, no one has remembered to wake up Bill and just as we set off Jane realises he is missing and finds him asleep in his car. So we leave without him, knowing that he will soon catch us up, which he does after about an hour. It is great that Richard is able to come along as his child is due to be born any day. He has a mobile phone with him so he can be called if his wife goes into labour. With local runners Andy, Bill and Richard doing this leg I again do not need to worry about the navigation until Yewbarrow, which is strange for me and Tom, who lives in Yorkshire, as in fell races it's normally us doing the navigation with others following!

As we climb out of the Ennerdale valley we emerge from the clouds and are treated to the beautiful view of them filling the valley with wisps coming and going over the tops. On long endurance events dawn is a special time, the light is often magical and the new day lifts the spirits. As I get going the pain in my knees vanishes and I forget the effort of the previous day; I am looking forward to a lovely day on the fells with my friends. The humidity seems to have dropped and the temperature is pleasant for running. We make great progress over the rocky tops, including the highest one of the section – the out and back to Pillar. As we approach Yewbarrow we see Al Lee and Rob Jarman again.

Al Lee: *'After spending the night trying to sleep in Rob's van we got up early to film Steve on Yewbarrow. As we approached the summit the path flattened off and there was the spectacular shot I was hoping for with Wasdale filled with clouds and the Scafells behind looking amazing. However, half an hour before Steve appeared Yewbarrow summit clouded over. I filmed Steve when he appeared but it could have been anywhere. All that effort carrying the heavy camera equipment up a mountain was again wasted, I was gutted and tired. I hoped things would be better on the Scafells where I was planning to next meet Steve.'*

The route from Yewbarrow to Seatallan is one that no one takes direct – there are no paths, just classic Lake District terrain. A mixture of big rocks, scree, grass, bracken and heather, some climbs, some descent and a bit of contouring. I have reccied the route, but with the cloud down and visibility down to fifty metres it all looks different to what I remember. We get our maps and compasses out and check we are going the right way. The bracken covering the rocks makes progress quite slow and we are tentative, but we find a good line and eventually start the big climb up to the summit of Seatallan – it is a relief not to have made a mistake. The final top on the section is Buckbarrow which is directly above Joss Naylor's house. There are two possible descent routes from this top; I go for the one I know which comes out on the road a kilometre and a half west of Joss's house, rather than the other route that goes straight past his house, but I forget to tell anyone to knock on his door so he doesn't know we have passed so close by.

Jane has done some more organisation wizardry and arranged for us to meet in the farmyard of the Wasdale Rare Goats Farm. It is great running in and seeing Emma and the children. As I sit down and take my shoes off they show me all the Father's Day cards and presents they have carefully made and bought for me. It is touching that they are missing me so much and so happy to see me, and also that Emma has found the time to help them make the cards. Matthew's card says inside it 'Have a nice time doing the Wainwrights'.

Emma: *'Me, James, Matthew and Hannah drove up to Woodhow in Wasdale in the morning (to me it is still my school friend Anita Lancaster's farm even though it has now been a goat farm for years). The lack of sleep must be getting to me as I left the handbrake half on and arrive with a smell of burning and with the brakes not working as well as they should. This is not good news as I am due to drive up Hardknott Pass (the steepest road in the Lake District) later in the day. I do not say anything to anyone as they do not need any extra worry. Just to add to the stress the children then decide to have a massive argument about who will open the gate for Steve when he arrives at Woodhow. Alison Herberts, being a mother of three children herself, can see the problem and sorts them out, for which I am eternally grateful. It is good to see Steve running a lot better and happy to see his Father's Day cards and presents. His support team have done a great job and Karen and Dan, his sister and brother-in-law,*

are supporting the next section. They know him and the fells really well
so he can't be in better hands. Things are looking up!'

SECTION 5	Wasdale Rare Goats Farm Yard to Hardknott Pass
DETAIL	31.1km, 3,030m ascent, 14 Wainwrights
SUPPORT TEAM	Karen and Dan Parker, and, for part of the section,
	Nic Barber, Mark Roberts and Paul 'Corny' Cornforth
TIMES	Start time 12.16, end time 21.25, break at end of leg 00.10

This is another key section. At 31.1 kilometres it's not the longest, but with 3,030 metres of ascent it's nearly the most climbing of any section; it is also the steepest and rockiest of any section and includes England's highest top, Scafell Pike. I am looking forward to completing this section and moving on to easier, grassier ground, but first I need to complete it. It's great having my family along to help, although with only two of them they do not have space to fit the handy-cam in their rucksacks.

I have my first energy low point as we climb up Whin Rigg at the top of The Screes above Wast Water. Every step up the hill is hard work and I feel really wobbly and light-headed. I hope it is only a temporary blip. I have some Torq gels – needless to say I've gone off the bars after throwing up – hoping that if I keep eating and drinking I will get over it, but there is always the worry that I won't get over it and I will carry on being slow uphill for the rest of the week. Even when it starts to flatten off I am still going really slowly and not making up much ground on the walkers who are around. I am dreading the steep climb to Slight Side – 400 metres of ascent mostly on big tussocks of grass with no path. But I take it steady and I manage to keep up a reasonable speed. It is a relief to reach the summit without suffering a major 'bonk'. After the summit we head towards Scafell. Soon the drizzle starts, and we go into the clouds with visibility reduced to around ten metres. Luckily I know I can rely on Karen and Dan's excellent navigation. After Scafell we meet Al Lee and Rob Jarman again and I can see that Al is not happy.

Al Lee: *'We climbed up Scafell from Wasdale – our third big climb with heavy packs in twenty-four hours. First we climbed to Mickledore and then tried to go up Broad Stand. I climbed halfway up but as Rob is not a rock climber, the rock was really greasy and we had heavy packs, I decided not to risk killing ourselves by climbing any further. So I climbed back down and we went up Scafell by the East Buttress, which I know well from climbing. However, I was confused when we got on the plateau at the top and I could not remember exactly where the summit was. There was also no point in getting the camera out as it was too wet and entirely shrouded in mist. Eventually Steve appeared and I was really disappointed not to be able to film him going down the West Wall Traverse as the support team did not have the handy-cam.'*

The fastest way from Scafell to Lingmell is by the West Wall Traverse. This is a very interesting route through Scafell Crag. Firstly it is down a very steep rocky gully, then the traverse itself along a narrow ledge before a rocky descent down amongst the big boulders of Lord's Rake. In dry weather the descent is just about OK but in the wet it is fairly unpleasant. So we take our time as we descend knowing it is more important to stay safe and not worry about how long it takes. Karen bravely comes down despite hating it. Eventually we reach the bottom and in the mist we are happy to find the contouring path to Lingmell, but we have taken forty-eight minutes between Scafell and Lingmell rather than the twenty-seven minutes we are scheduled to take. This shows the weakness of my schedule, which does not take sufficient account of descents, and particularly rough descents.

After Lingmell the next top is Scafell Pike and it is up the main tourist path so easy going. However, as we reach the summit, I'm surprised to see Al and Rob are the only people there. Al gets some nice film of me talking on the summit cairn, reminding me that the summit is a quarter of the way round. I try to be positive and say that a quarter is nearly half

… but there is an awfully long way to go. However, Scafell Pike has always been my first aim and I have made it just twenty-five minutes behind schedule with no injuries or blisters. After this the terrain becomes easier, as I have deliberately planned it so the first quarter contains some of the roughest, toughest and longest sections.

> **Al Lee:** *'Although I got some decent footage of Steve on Scafell Pike, overall I was really disappointed. My morale was really bad. Steve had completed the most dramatic sections of his route and I only had a few short clips suitable for the film. Rob and I were shattered, dehydrated and short of sleep. So tired that as we descended to Wasdale I was convinced we were descending to Borrowdale until the cloud suddenly lifted to reveal our location. I really doubted I was going to be able to make a good film. I felt utterly defeated. I decided to go home to recover and think of a new plan.'*

On the summit I am joined by Corny, Mark and Nic. It's great to see these familiar faces again. It is nice to chat to them and they seem to know what I need without even asking. From the many fell races that go along the next summits they also know all the best lines through the massive boulders even though visibility is still down to ten metres. It's becoming obvious that the three guys are having a private battle between them to see who can do the most summits with me, so I will be seeing a lot more of them over the next five days. Rossett Pike was one of those tops that did not join up nicely with any other tops when I was planning the route. In the end the best place for it was between Esk Pike and Bow Fell. Unfortunately this entails a 300-metre very steep drop from Esk Pike, a small climb up to the summit, then a small descent back down from the summit, followed by a steep 300-metre climb back up amongst a massive boulder field to Bow Fell. The route back up Bow Fell is on the Bob Graham Round so the best line is well known, and although there is not a path there are a few cairns and some worn lines to show the way. The direct route down from Esk Pike is one that is very rarely taken as there are some big crags where it is easy to get stuck. After a bit of a discussion we decide not to risk the direct route, as the cloud is still down, but go round to the west of Angle Tarn which is a couple of minutes slower but the safe and sensible option.

After saying goodbye to Corny, Mark and Nic I again need to rely on Karen and Dan's navigation skills as the route off Cold Pike is not how I remember it, but they are spot on. It is 8 p.m. and the temperature is now beginning to drop. I put my shirt on as I am slightly chilly. The bad side of the low temperature is that there is now a heavy dew and my shoes get wet. It seems that thirty-six hours of my feet sweating profusely, which has softened and expanded my feet, together with them now getting cold and wet from the outside has made them really susceptible to blisters, and I get a small one on the little toe of my right foot. This is really annoying; I desperately want to avoid blisters at all costs. Along with being able to eat and drink, and not getting an injury, it is one of the key things on a run like this. You only have to read the accounts of Joss and Alan to see how painful and debilitating they can become. But now I have one despite changing my socks and shoes at each support point. Some people get loads of blisters but I am not one of them. In the Dragon's Back Race I had just one small one over five long days, so it is surprising to get one so soon. However, I have to accept it and we – me and the support team – just need to make sure we keep it under control, although there is no long rest period planned so little chance for it to recover.

Hardknott Pass is a quick stop – it is too steep for the campervans to get up here. Jean Sinclair brings up my new support team in her car and my family are there again, playing on the rocks and scaring everyone while waiting for me. I eat a bit of food, change my shoes and socks and then I am off again.

SECTION 6	Hardknott Pass to Duddon Road above Stepping Stones
DETAIL	9km, 420m ascent, 2 Wainwrights
SUPPORT TEAM	Ryan Wood, Peter Murphy and Steph Scott
TIMES	Start time 21.35, end time 23.28, break at end of leg 05.08

I am desperate to get off quickly, as navigation on the next section worries me – Joss lost an hour or so in this area in the dark and I want to get as much of it done in daylight as possible. It gets properly dark as we descend from Harter Fell, Pete leads the way and once we are descending on the right path I tell him it is easy and we cannot go wrong. But it is soon clear that we are going in slightly the wrong direction and not heading for the corner of the forest, which is where we should be going. So we have to contour across rough, heathery, rocky ground to get back to the correct path. I think that maybe I should stop giving advice and let my support crew find the way! After the corner of the forest it is fairly flat through some peat groughs and knee-deep tussocks. There is a bit of a line that I have reccied, which twists and turns and avoids the worst of the groughs and tussocks, but as I expected we cannot find it in the dark. So Pete goes ahead and scouts a decent line and eventually we are through the worst section and on to the grassier section for an out-and-back up to the summit of Green Crag. It is now drizzling and I am feeling a bit cold, my feet are soaking wet again and the blister is getting quite sore. Steph waits at the end of a sheep trod through the tussocks that will lead us back in the correct direction after we have been up the summit, while I go to the summit with Pete and Ryan. Annoyingly, Steph's trod through the tussocks disappears after a while so we have to follow Pete while he scouts a route through the tussocks. I am very relieved when we arrive at the forest edge in exactly the correct place.

After crossing the Duddon river by the stepping stones we see the vans but no one is out – I wonder why? However, as soon as we stop the reason is immediately obvious. The midges are absolutely horrendous, by far the worst I have ever experienced in England. Any bare flesh imme-diately turns black as thousands fly on to the skin. Jane pushes us into the campervan but we bring in thousands of the horrible creatures with us. I have a Torq recovery drink and some food that Emma made at her par-ents' house and took to Hardknott Pass, while Jean Sinclair deals with my blister. As I did not get any sleep the previous night I plan on lying down as soon as possible and getting four hours, but again it does not work out. The midges we have brought into the campervan have bitten my feet and they are agony. I want to avoid any more bites by covering them up, but I also want to leave my feet uncovered to let them dry. I decide of the two evils it is best not to let the midges bite my feet so I cover them up. My knees are throbbing again and together with the midge bites I lie there in pain, shattered, and desperate to sleep but failing miserably.

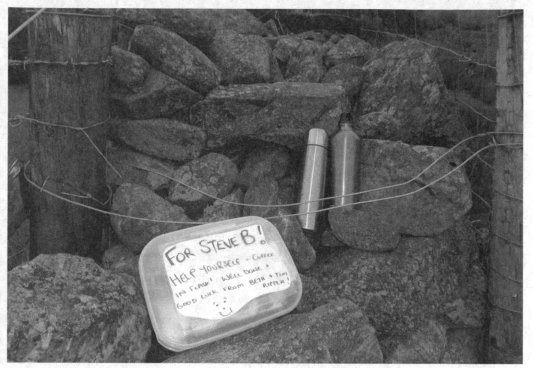

Food and drink placed out for me (from someone not on my support team) as I pass through the Duddon Valley.
Photo: Steve Birkinshaw Collection.

20 DAY THREE

SECTION 7   Duddon Road above Stepping Stones to Tilberthwaite
             Quarry Car Park
DETAIL   15.1km, 1,230m ascent, 7 Wainwrights
SUPPORT TEAM Chris Knowles, Ryan Wood and
             Peter Murphy
TIMES   Start time 04.36, end time 08.08, break at end of leg 00.17

The guys are waiting patiently for me outside, being badly bitten by the midges, while I slowly get ready. Eventually I stumble out of the van ready to go and they start running with me. I feel like an arrogant movie star that everyone has to wait on, but no one ever grumbles, they just get on with it and seem happy to help in any way they can. I am so lucky to have such a great team supporting me.

Soon after starting we pass some food and drink someone has left for me on a wall which says 'for Steve' on it. It is great to know people are tracking my progress and keen to help in any way possible. We decide to take the track up to Walna Scar pass and then on to Dow Crag rather than the straight grassy route. It is further but I can get a good rhythm with the poles on the hard surface. We have started out one hour and thirty minutes behind schedule from the Duddon valley, but pick up twenty-three minutes to Dow Crag and seven minutes more up Coniston Old Man. It is an absolutely perfect morning to be out running, cool and dry and with great visibility. At 6 a.m., soon after Coniston Old Man, the phone Chris is carrying rings. It is Emma, she is following the tracker and it clearly shows we have missed out Dow Crag. She wants to catch us before we go any further so we can go back and do it; I do not want to get a record for completing 213 Wainwrights. She is extremely relieved to learn that we *did* in fact go over Dow Crag.

Peter Murphy: 'I can confirm that we definitely DID go over Dow Crag! The route the tracker shows is no short cut, it'd be a hell of a lot harder than the real one that we took! I've even got video evidence of the route – I was getting a bit arty-farty and trying to capture the sun rising through the wisps of mist that were still hanging around; it was beautiful and a great privilege to be up there at such an hour.'

Jane: 'As soon as we left the Duddon valley and had mobile reception again my phone went mad. There were loads of calls and texts worrying that Steve had gone the wrong way. I talked to Emma and she let me know it was the tracker that was wrong. It took a couple of hours to contact everyone and let them know what had happened.'

James Thurlow: 'I've switched the tracker so the GPS is now on all the time. Previously it switched on each time it sent an update – I think it may use a bit more battery but will keep an eye on it. I can see from the

data that the GPS strength was poor for that section. Hopefully my tweak
should prevent it happening again.'

The blister on my big toe – I have several now – is really sore as we descend Wetherlam. We stop and put on some Compeed for the descent to the support point at Tilberthwaite. I am worried about this descent as it is a route I have never taken before but we are lucky it is a great grassy line and we reach the support point only forty-six minutes behind schedule and best of all there are no midges to annoy me! Jean does a great job of sorting us out and we are gone in seventeen minutes. I wonder how Chris and Ryan will get back to their cars but I decide it is not worth worrying about; Jane and my support crew have got it all brilliantly sorted so I can just forget about it and concentrate on moving quickly.

SECTION 8 — Tilberthwaite Quarry Car Park to New Dungeon Ghyll, Langdale
DETAIL — 12.7km, 800m ascent, 3 Wainwrights
SUPPORT TEAM — David 'Dexter' Armstrong and Peter Murphy
TIMES — Start time 08.25, end time 11.15, break at end of leg 00.30

This section has only three small Wainwrights. Strangely the navigation is actually some of the hardest of the entire run. There is a real mixture of fell, plantation forests, native forest, fields and walls. Some of it is open-access land, where you are allowed anywhere, and some is not, so you can only go on public footpaths. I reccied most of it in the spring; unfortunately the bracken is now fully grown and two metres tall in places, which makes the going much slower.

I decide to change from my Inov-8 X-Talons to my Hokas to see if different shoes will help with my blisters and also as there are some road sections. It is nice to have a bit more cushioning but it does not seem to be any less painful on my blisters. In a nice secluded bit of forest I stop for a poo (only my second of the run …) and I am happy that my bowels seem to be working OK. However, I am put off by Pete wanting to *film* me … I eventually persuade him not to. Apart from the first day my wee is also regular and pale coloured, which is great – I am clearly staying properly hydrated. I am frustrated that I am struggling to run along a flat road – I must be getting tired, but I am keeping to schedule so it is OK. The final descent of the section from Lingmoor I have not reccied. Pete does his scouting duties again and finds the best line down. The line I have drawn on the map looks really rough so I am glad we don't go that way. A jet zooms down the valley as we approach the bottom. Dexter says that they have come to see me, but although I am tired I am not that easily fooled.

I have a real treat in store for me at Langdale. The support point is at the Langdale bunkhouse, which Ben Turner runs, and it is also right next to his house so he lets me use his shower. It's amazing how much difference having a nice warm shower makes – two days of mud and sweat is cleaned off and I feel refreshed. Emma has also brought along some home-made soup and bread which goes down very well. Meanwhile Jean is again doing a great job of sorting out the blisters on my feet; she has lots of experience of doing this at other races, such as the Dragon's Back Race, and the rest of the support crew are very happy they don't have to do it.

When I worked out my schedule I always found the timings for Section 10 difficult. The problem was that it was an eight-hour section and I could either put it straight after Section 9, starting at 8 p.m. and so finishing it at 4 a.m., or have a four-hour break after Section 9 and so start at midnight and finish at 8 a.m. I liked neither option, as I would be out between midnight and 4 a.m., which ideally is when I wanted to be sleeping. It's a natural time to be asleep, so if I was out I would expect to be drowsy and moving slower, and in addition to this, finding the perfect lines over terrain is hard in the dark. What I thought would happen is that I would get either ahead of or behind my schedule so the decision would be easy. But when I arrive in Langdale at the end of Section 8, after going for over two days, I am only twenty-five minutes behind.

So I do not know which of the two options to take. It will make sorting out everything so much easier for my support team if they have a definite decision. After a shower and a decent meal I feel good so suggest I might want to carry straight on after Section 9 but I am still not sure. My indecision is a real headache for Jane and the team.

SECTION 9	New Dungeon Ghyll, Langdale to Rydal Church
DETAIL	35.2km, 2,150m ascent, 18 Wainwrights
SUPPORT TEAM	Ben Turner, David 'Dexter' Armstrong and, for part of the section, Gavin Bland
TIMES	Start time 11.45, end time 19.46, break at end of leg 05.24

It is lovely to have Emma joining us for the start of this section. It is also great to have Ben along as he trains in the Langdale Pikes every day and so we can enjoy the views without having to worry about going the correct way. Once we have done the hard initial climb there are five Wainwrights – the Langdale Pikes – very close together, with little effort needed to get between them, and it is nice to tick them off so easily. After Sergeant Man we get some more expert knowledge as Gavin Bland, British fell running champion in 1999 and nephew of Billy Bland, is waiting for us. His sheep farm includes these fells and so he seems to know every blade of grass. He leaves us at Steel Fell just above his farm. I am worried about the big climb up Tarn Crags but I keep moving at a steady pace. There is now plenty of movement in my bowels and unfortunately for Ben and Dexter my farts are really smelly. Ben teaches me the adventure racing technique of raising my arm to warn those following of what is happening. I become an expert at this over the rest of this section. The run to Silver How seems to go very slowly in the heat of the afternoon as the path wanders around lumps. However, seeing orienteering friend Mike Pearson – who also helped Joss twenty-eight years ago – on top with some food and drink cheers me up.

I am getting very tired and so despite knowing the descent off Silver How I get it wrong and we have to cut back a bit. Eventually we reach Red Bank where I miss the tourist path up Loughrigg so go up the fell race route. It is incredibly hot climbing and I am feeling very dehydrated and glad this section is nearly finished. *The Fellrunner* magazine editor, Britta Sendlhofer, is waiting for us on top, which is great, as Loughrigg is a maze of paths between high bracken and she directs us down the correct path towards Rydal.

At the support point we are now fifteen minutes up on schedule and lots of people are waiting for us. I am feeling really tired, so I decide that instead of continuing straight on to Section 10 I will have a long rest and sleep here.

> Jane: *'We didn't know if Steve was going to have a long rest here. But if he decided to rest then our planned support point on the track to Rydal Hall was going to be too steep for him to sleep. So Charles Scott went to Rydal Hall and they were very helpful in arranging a permit for us to use a nearby flat car park. When Steve decided to rest we explained to the support runners that they now had five hours to wait until Steve was going to leave but everyone was great and accepted it without any complaints. A couple of support runners went to the pub and a couple we fed and they had a bit of a rest in their cars.'*

My knees start throbbing really badly as soon as I lie down in the campervan and they stop me going to sleep again. I am becoming very frustrated by this; I desperately want to sleep, I am exhausted, but the pain in my knees is stopping it from happening. Dr Alison Scott comes into the campervan and tries some breathing techniques with me, which relaxes me but I am still awake. Phil Davies does some massage and then some traction work on my legs, which seems to reduce the pain. Finally I get some deep sleep, maybe a couple of hours, although not the four I was hoping for.

Mel Culleton-Wright: *'I joined the support team here, taking over from Jean Sinclair with the job of looking after Steve's feet. I thought that with my experience as an accident and emergency nurse and a medic, patching up feet on the 2012 Dragon's Back Race, I would have a significant role to play. After three very long days his feet were now in a bad way. He had six blisters (three on each foot), both feet were completely macerated underneath and there was a minor infection making them itchy. Maceration leaves the skin white and soft, vulnerable to breakdown and infection, and painful to run on – a disaster waiting to happen. This condition was caused by constantly wet feet, due to running on wet ground and sweating caused by the high temperatures and humidity. I now had a stark reality check. Keeping his feet in a runnable condition and monitoring his physical well-being were now my main priorities over the next four days. What I did to his feet could, at best, make his record-breaking journey more comfortable and at worst, promote failure. At this point it was paramount to remove the wet shoes, socks and dressings and to cover his feet in talc to get them dry before he had some sleep. I hoped the talc would speed up the drying process. Thankfully it did, and after a few hours I was cleaning off the talc and getting his feet ready to run. The new dressings had to survive several hours of constant running through mud, water, wet grass and up and down mountains while being bombarded with sweat and constant movement over every kind of terrain. Steve's feet had to stay runnable for another four days.'*

Shoes laid out for my arrival. My shoe selection is crucial, it depends on the terrain on the next section and how sore it will be on my blisters. Photo: Steve Birkinshaw Collection.

21   DAY FOUR

SECTION 10   Rydal Church to Kirkstone Pass
DETAIL   28.4km, 2,320m ascent, 15 Wainwrights
SUPPORT TEAM   Chris Knowles, Jeff Powell Davies, Mark Roberts and Phil Davies
TIMES   Start time 01.10, end time 07.41, break at end of leg 00.59

Having moved Section 10 to day four this is going to be a crucial day. I now have four sections, with the plan to set off at 1 a.m. and finish twenty-three hours later at midnight. This makes a daily total of ninety-two kilometres with 6,200 metres of ascent, so around eighty-five to ninety per cent of a Bob Graham Round. This is going to be hard having already completed three long days; if I can get through this day I might just about be able to complete this challenge.

It is actually quite pleasant to be setting off in the cool night air and there is something quite therapeutic about following a narrow beam of light.

I set off in my Hokas but the guys are carrying a pair of X-Talons with them in case it gets too rough for the Hokas. They are also carrying four pairs of socks so I can change them every two hours with the plan that my feet can stay as dry as possible and the maceration and infection can improve. The guys have been looking at the map while waiting for me for five hours and have realised that it makes more sense to take Stone Arthur before Greatrigg Man rather than the other way round, which I had planned to do. I have a look at the map and agree with them so we do what they suggest.

The contouring trod through the rocks to the col before Seat Sandal is hard to find and we miss it in the dark. I think we are too low but we are actually too high. I realise I am too tired to make sensible route choices and it is definitely time to shut up and let my support team choose all the routes. I am glad I do, as when we descend to the col before Hart Crag we take a slightly different and better route to my normal one.

There is a gradual lightening of the sky as we do the out-and-back to Hartsop above How, but instead of the previous morning when it was bright and sunny, this morning it is quite grey. It is a shame that the views will be less beautiful but the conditions are cool and perfect for running. In fact it soon gets quite cold and I need to stop to put some more clothes on.

Soon after getting going again I feel some tendonitis pain in my right leg at the front of my ankle. It is in the same place but on the other leg to the problem I got during the fourth day of the Dragon's Back Race. Then I managed to run for a day and a half with it, but the day after I finished I could barely walk. I am very worried because I have over three and a half days to go. Will this be the problem that causes me to stop, pull out in agony and not achieve my goal? I wonder if it is my shoes so I change from my Hokas to my X-Talons, but the tendonitis is still painful for the rest of the section.

After two more out-and-backs we eventually reach Red Screes. I struggle with my coordination on the descent but we make good progress down the racing line to the Kirkstone Inn, where I arrive twenty-six minutes up on schedule. This is the halfway point, which is really important psychologically as from now on I will be counting down Wainwrights not counting up. The good news is that I am on schedule but the bad news is that I have bad blisters and tendonitis in one leg. I am moving OK, but what if the pain gets worse? Can I carry on coping with the pain and push myself onwards? Realistically, I think I am probably not going to be able to do this. But I need to get these negative thoughts out of my mind. I need to stay positive. I have loads of experience – I know there will be bad patches. I need to remember Joss's advice – just break it down into bits rather than think of the entire route. I need to split it into days, then into sections, then into the next climb or descent, then into the next step. I have to think about each and every step as progress towards the final goal.

I receive lots of treatment on my feet from Mel and at the same time I get a massage from Phil. Mel is happy the maceration and infection seem to be showing some signs of improvement and Phil works the muscles around the tendonitis and does some more traction work. I manage to eat and drink while they are doing this, except when the treatment is making me scream in agony. Instead of an individual effort, this is turning more and more into a massive team effort, of people going out of their way to look after my every need and helping me complete this challenge.

SECTION 11	Kirkstone Pass to Troutbeck (Lay-by on Road before Limefitt Caravan Park)
DETAIL	22.3km, 1,430m ascent, 9 Wainwrights
SUPPORT TEAM	Andy Thompson, Joe Faulkner and Nic Davies
TIMES	Start time 08.40, end time 13.22, break at end of leg 00.36

After sitting in the campervan for an hour it seems really cool when we leave and I put on my Berghaus down jacket to stop me shivering. After ten minutes I am feeling warm again so I take it off and throw it at someone without any explanation or a 'please can you look after this'. I am beginning to get used to people doing everything for me and not complaining about it.

Joe – running with me now – helped support Joss Naylor on a section twenty-eight years ago, so it is nice to have him here with me, but he has a cold so he makes sure I do not get too close to him. As well as Joe, Andy and Nic, someone else who has been following the tracker joins us for most of the section but although I talk to him for a couple of hours and he tells me his name several times my memory is now so bad I cannot remember what it is. Andy is surprised how well I am still going after three long days and together with the route being mainly on short grass or big paths I pick up a bit of time on my schedule. However, the steep descent from Yoke towards Troutbeck Tongue is really sore on my tendonitis; the angle of my foot on each step seems to be perfect for irritating it. As it is grassy we think it would be suitable for sliding down and luckily Nic has some waterproof overtrousers which just about fit. So I slide down on my bottom, although I am careful to avoid the big rocks.

It is getting very warm again as we ascend Wansfell, the final peak on this section, but once we are over the summit I manage to run the long descent from there to Troutbeck. About five minutes before the support point I see a guy in work clothes standing by the roadside, which seems a bit strange. Then I realise it is Jo Scott, who first put the idea in my mind of doing all the Wainwrights. He has an hour off on his lunch break so has come along to join me, chatting as we run along the road. Emma has managed to do a bit of work in Kendal and has come to see me on her lunch break. I am now thirty-one minutes up on schedule and I am happy to have a decent break and follow my normal regime of foot treatment and lots of food and drink.

Emma: *'I was mad to think I could still go to work for three days this week and help out for a day on James's residential. Steve had said "don't worry, the team of helpers can look after me, you just have to look after the children" so I thought it would be fine just to call in and say hello now and again then get back to my life. Most of the time when he does long runs I am not around as he is running somewhere a long way from home. I have also never been into the waiting-for-hours-just-to-see-him-run-past thing; it's boring and to be honest, having been a keen runner myself I find it pretty frustrating and would rather be doing something else. Besides, the children just don't do waiting around. I wonder where they get that from?! However, this was different; Steve needed me and the kids where feasible for some kind of moral support, so we had to do the best we could to get to the support points. I manage to head down to Kendal after school drop-off and do almost a day's work. Luckily my colleagues at the Lake District National Park are really understanding and have been follow-ing Steve on the tracker and Claire, my boss, has allowed me to fit work in where and when I can, knowing I will make up any lost time in future weeks. I rush into Kendal Asda and 'Supermarket Sweep' style buy every pack of Compeed in the shop. I pay at the self-service checkouts as anyone serving me would think it was a bit weird. I get to Troutbeck just in time to see Steve arrive; the blisters are bothering him and he seems quite low. He does not say much but at least with Mel, the superstar nurse, he is in safe hands to keep his blisters under control.'*

SECTION 12	**Troutbeck to Kentmere (High Lane)**
DETAIL	**7.4km, 490m ascent, 2 Wainwrights**
SUPPORT TEAM	**Andy Thompson and Nick Ray**
TIMES	**Start time 13.58, end time 15.27, break at end of leg 00.58**

This is the shortest section of the whole route with only two Wainwrights and 7.4 kilometres. The only difficulty on the route is finding the best way up to Sour Howes. Nick knows a good line that is different from the one I have reccied but I am happy to follow him. It is now very hot and I am very grateful for the shady section in a forest for five minutes. I feel shattered as I descend into Kentmere but I run OK down the hill.

I'm now taking regular doses of paracetamol and ibuprofen. However, the nurses and doctors only let me have it if I am properly hydrated. So every time I finish a section the first questions asked are 'When did you last have a wee?' and 'What colour was it?' I have someone in charge of drugs on each section. They make sure I don't have any more than the recommended dosages – by this stage I am too tired to remember when I last had any painkillers.

I spend a while in Kentmere, I know that what is coming up is a crucial eight-hour section at the end of a long day, and if all goes to plan I will finish around midnight at Martindale. I am having a mid-afternoon dip and feel very sleepy; it's hot outside the campervan – great for sunbathing but not for running. The thought of a long, hard afternoon and evening running on sore feet fills me with dread. But I *must* get out and start moving again.

Emma: *'This is the worst I've seen him so far. The blisters are horrible and he is dreading the next long leg into the night. I had intended to go home earlier, but having seen him at the previous support point at Troutbeck I kind of thought he might be struggling here, not that there is much I can do. Luckily Steve's mum picked up Hannah from school and our friend Mady Thompson is looking after Matthew, so I can stay out a little longer. Kentmere is looking beautiful and it's a lovely afternoon, but still not tempting to run for eight hours on blisters. Dr Joyce Woffindin, who is an orienteering friend, is there and suggests stronger painkillers, so gives the support team some tablets with added codeine, with strict instructions to give it to him towards the end of the leg. He sets off in the end but doesn't look good. I cannot see how he can keep going to the end in this state, in my head the odds of him finishing have now dropped to ten per cent.'*

SECTION 13	Kentmere (High Lane) to Martindale Church
DETAIL	34.3km, 1,940m ascent, 17 Wainwrights
SUPPORT TEAM	Nick Ray, Nic Barber, Andrew Davies and, for part of the section, Paul 'Corny' Cornforth, Mark Roberts, Gavin Bland and Graham Watson
TIMES	Start time 16.25, end time 23.57, break at end of leg 05.16

By this stage I have no idea who will be supporting me on the next section. Some of the people were in the schedule but there have been lots of changes. Jane sorts it all out and I just see who is there. Andrew Davies arrived back from Portugal earlier in the day and he has been roped in to help. Nick Ray was planned to help, but these two are also joined again by Nic Barber and Mark Roberts.

Jane: *'Earlier in the day I told Steve we were sorted for support runners for this section (so he did not worry) but in fact we only had Nick lined up, and one runner was going to be completely insufficient for such a long and crucial leg. I spent a lot of the day on the phone trying to cajole and encourage support runners for Steve. I eventually got through to Gavin Bland and he said he had really stiff and tired legs from helping Steve yesterday but would try and come out. The others I rang up were willing to come out as Gavin was making the effort, even though he was suffering. In the end there were lots of support runners, which was good, but it is hard to know who will turn up at the last moment. Over the week I also spent a lot of the time on the phone talking to James Thurlow about the trackers and Steve's location. Mobile reception was not good enough for the support team to follow the position of Steve's tracker on the map, so I would ring up James and ask where Steve was and when he expected him to finish that section.'*

When I eventually leave the comfort of the campervan we start moving slowly, but I still seem to be keeping to schedule, which is good news. We go up two new Wainwrights for me: Tarn Crag and Grey Crag. But the terrain here is not particularly inspiring, mostly marshy and tussocky, I probably will not be coming back again any time soon. Gavin Bland appears and joins us for the rest of the section and his stories keep us all amused as we move steadily along.

At Gatescarth Pass we move from a wet section to a dry rocky section, so we have a planned stop for a change of socks and shoes to keep my feet dry and stop the maceration reappearing. The midges are exceptionally annoying and start to bite as soon as we stop, so I quickly get my dry shoes on and set off. The new socks feel really nice and comfortable but one of the shoes starts to hurt immediately on the outside of my heel – it's pressing directly on to my blister. I am in *extreme pain* now when I put my foot down – rather than the usual *lots of pain*. We try and think about what to do and someone says that Joss Naylor recommends using sheep wool between the blisters and the shoe. It is worth a try but up on the ridge we can only find a small bit and it does not help. We find a big bit of deer wool but that does not help either.

Eventually the pain gets to be too much for me, and as I climb Mardale Ill Bell I take off my shoes and throw them to the ground. I walk uphill with just my socks on as we climb the pitched rock path. This is an amazing relief as there is no pain as I walk. Unfortunately the pitched path does not last long and soon we are on to a typical Lake District path covered with small, loose spiky stones, which I cannot walk over with just socks on. We decide it is best to see if we can burst the blister. Andrew and Gavin remove the bandages and we can see the blister is full of pus, but we have nothing to burst it with. Gavin asks if any of us have a safety pin. Eventually Nick finds a rusty old one at the bottom of his rucksack. Gavin then bursts the blister and says 'That's it! Beauty!' as it drains out. They put the bandages and my shoe back on and we get going again.

There is pain when I am running but it is now manageable compared to the agony beforehand. This is an amazing relief, I could not have carried on for long with that pain but now it is still possible I can do this.

Soon after the shoe incident Graham Watson runs towards us along the High Street ridge and joins us for the rest of the section. He says he has just seen a paraglider with a motor on it.

Al Lee: *'After the extremely bad first two days trying to film Steve, I returned home really dejected. I felt a lot better once I had rested and recovered. From home I could also easily follow the tracker (whereas in the Lake District with poor mobile reception this was impossible). Steve was obviously still going well and I could also see the online interest via social media growing rapidly. I decided on a new plan: to take to the air. So I contacted Paul Haxby, although I had never met him. I knew he had a paraglider with a motor on the back. I sorted out a large field at a campsite near Pooley Bridge on the edge of Ullswater for him to take off and land in and we met there on the evening of Steve's fourth day. I gave Paul my really expensive uninsured camera equipment and he set off to try and film Steve and his support team. Taking off looked quite alarming, as he had to run the length of the field before he got enough speed to get into the air. After three hours Paul returned wet and cold having been up in the clouds. Unfortunately things did not go to plan again as he failed to find Steve.'*

We make really good progress along the High Street ridge. I manage to run all the descents and most of the flat sections. But with the sun going down as we approach Arthur's Pike I feel completely shattered and my knees are getting very sore. We walk the short distance from Arthur's Pike to Bonscale Pike but time seems to be dragging. It feels like thirty minutes but is actually only sixteen. We have just a long descent and a short climb to the campervans and the end of the day. I have reccied the start of the descent but mess it up again and I have to cut back to a couple of the guys who have gone the correct way – when will I ever learn that I am too tired to make navigational decisions!

The plan is to take the codeine around thirty minutes before we finish the section, so the effect kicks in just as we arrive at the campervan. The hope is that it will enable me to have a good sleep as the strong painkilling effect will stop my knees aching and the drug's side effect of drowsiness will also help. So on the steep descent I take the codeine but it kicks in a bit early on the short climb back to the campervan. I start talking complete rubbish and wobbling from side to side half asleep. I suddenly stop caring. The guys are very worried I will either stop beside the track and go to sleep or fall over and hurt myself. So they decide to have one of them walking on each side of me, telling me exactly what to do and making sure I carry on moving. Eventually we reach the campervan but I do not really remember anything apart from feeling like I am very drunk. I have not had any codeine for over twenty years and obviously it has quite an effect on me. Dr Joyce decides that next time I should have a lower dose! Maybe just half a tablet …

Emma: 'As Steve's mum, Sue, is staying in our house I can head out in the night to Martindale Church once the children are asleep. Steve is completely spaced out by the time he arrives and looks drunk with the tiredness and the codeine, but relieved he has managed that long leg. Lots of things are hurting though. I have brought food I have cooked and clothes that I have washed and dried.'

Leaving Patterdale with Emma offering encouragement. I am well over halfway but still have nearly 200 kilometres to go. Photo: Steve Birkinshaw Collection.

22   DAY FIVE

SECTION 14	Martindale Church to Patterdale White Lion Inn
DETAIL	18.3km 1,540m ascent, 8 Wainwrights
SUPPORT TEAM	Kim Collinson, Graham Watson and Jim Davies
TIMES	Start time 05.13, end time 09.59, break at end of leg 01.00

Emma: *'I think Steve slept OK for three or four hours, or maybe I was so tired I didn't notice. By now everything is a bit of a blur of sleeping and waking for all of the support team; I call people the wrong name and can't remember basic details like which day of the week we are on. Jane has got to the point where she feels she is not safe driving so Alison Herberts and Charles Scott do the driving from now on. It is a lovely morning, but Steve can hardly walk, hobbling along with his sticks like an old man. How on earth is he going to finish now? I drive back home in time to get the children up and to school.'*

Stepping out of the campervan is *agony*. I feel sleepy, my muscles are sore and all my joints feel really stiff. But a lot worse than any of that is the pain in my feet. Both feet have three blisters and the shoes pressing against each of them causes me to yelp in pain, and at that moment the last thing I want to do is spend another long day on the fells. I hobble about ten paces and then pull my shoes off and throw them to the ground. Without shoes I make steady progress up the short grassy climb to the top of Hallin Fell. From the top I have to go back down the same way to the campervan and then continue on to the next fell, Steel Knotts. I put my shoes back on at the top and hobble back as quickly as I can to the campervan. Meanwhile Charles Scott realises I need some different shoes, so instead of climbing with me all the way to the top of Hallin Fell, when we get to about halfway up he runs down. Then together with the rest of the support team they get out all my shoes (having just packed them away) and on my return to the campervan I select another pair of the X-Talons. These are still agony but a lesser form of agony.

The climb to Steel Knotts is rough. Kim Collison works for the Outward Bound nearby so takes a good route. However, my mind is full of negative thoughts. Although I am nearly on schedule I know I am moving slowly. I am losing minutes on every fell and I still have 220 kilo-metres to go. I have seen it many times in adventure races and when helping on Bob Graham Rounds where people start to go slower and slower and it is not long before they are well behind schedule and they eventually drop out. I could see it happening to me, being slowly ground down by the pain and the gradual realisation that I would not be able to achieve my goal. This downward spiral of negative thoughts continues as we climb and then descend Beda Fell. The rough bracken-covered slopes cause a slight twist every time I put my feet down and with it another shriek of pain. I start to think how much more of this I can take and wonder if it will not be long before I give up. I don't say anything, but carry on thinking that I am now just going through the motions rather than actually believing I can do it. I think about all the people who have helped and how I will let them down. I think of my family, and how I could have spent more time with them rather than out training trying to achieve a stupid goal. I think of Jane Saul, and how she has taken two weeks off work to help me. I think of the fifty-plus people who have turned up to help me over the week. Then I think of the money I am raising for the MS charities and how it will now not be very much. I feel sad.

The 400-metre climb up to The Nab is covered in bracken and very steep. I keep looking at my altimeter to work out how much climbing I have to do. Then I start to set myself little targets, and see if I can climb fifteen metres in the next minute. I succeed, so I see if I can climb fifteen metres the minute after. I then try to climb at that rate all the way to the top. I look at my support team. Jim and Kim are two of the country's top fell runners and I can see they are working hard – they are also carrying big rucksacks with all my kit in – and I am slightly dropping Graham, who is a good fell runner. I know that normally over this sort of terrain I try to climb at twenty metres per minute and to be climbing only a little slower on my fifth day is brilliant, especially as on my schedule at this stage I was down to only eight metres per minute. I succeed in my aim of climbing all the way to the summit at fifteen metres per minute; I have picked up loads of time. The negative downward spiral has gone. I suddenly feel positive. I think of the rest of the section and realise the descents are mostly on grassy or rocky paths and my blisters feel less sore on these surfaces and so I know I can jog these descents. The rest of the day also has mostly grassy and rocky paths. Maybe I *can* do this.

Jim Davies: *'The first hour was slow and obviously very painful for Steve. He often complained about his sore feet and legs, but then the complaining stopped, the pace picked up and Steve was chatty and fo-cused on the running. He was climbing strongly, a little slower on the de-scents and struggling with rough terrain. This is Steve's fifth day of running and anyone covering this sort of distance will hurt from overuse injuries and there is very little that can be done about it.'*

Al Lee: *'Paul Haxby had another go at finding and filming Steve from his motorised paraglider. He set off at 5 a.m. By 9 a.m. he had not returned and I was very worried as he only had two to three hours of fuel. I thought it was quite possible he had crashed and was lying somewhere badly injured. I was just about to call the mountain rescue when he jumped over a wall and ran towards me really hot and sweaty. He had run out of fuel and landed in a farmer's field. The farmer shouted at him for landing in his field and scaring his animals with the noise. So he quickly left, hid his parachute and ran back along the road to Pooley Bridge. He was very happy to have captured some great film of Steve and his support team.'*

After leaving Martindale at the start of the section one hour behind schedule, with my fast climbing I have actually picked up forty minutes and so arrive at Patterdale only twenty minutes down. Jane has arranged for Gillian Beggs and Tom Driscoll from the Patterdale post office to make their home available for me, so I can have a shower before moving to their front room where Mel can treat my battered feet and Jim can give me a massage. It is amazing the difference a shower and sitting in a comfy chair eating lots of nice food (soup, nuts, crisps) makes. Afterwards I feel refreshed and ready to go again. Meanwhile, Jane has also arranged for the rest of the team to sort out everything in the White Lion pub car park while Ally from the pub checks over the campervan, which seems to have an oil problem.

Jane: *'Steve now has only two pairs of shoes he likes. A pair of X-Talons in size eleven and one in size eleven and a half. He wants a pair of size 12. So I rang up Pete Bland Sports and sent Steve's mum to Kendal (a two-hour round trip) to collect them. We also managed to borrow a pair of undertakers' shoe stretchers from Tom Driscoll and used these on* *the wet shoes at the end of every section. Steve has used all twenty-four pairs of new socks but, as usual with washed socks that have been worn on the fells, they came back with bits in. We tried to remove all the bits by hand but we could not get them all out so I rang Berghaus to ask for a delivery of new socks.'*

SECTION 15	Patterdale White Lion Inn to Glenridding Greenside Mine Road
DETAIL	16.5km, 1,410m ascent, 8 Wainwrights
SUPPORT TEAM	Bill Stewart, Kim Collinson and Jane Meeks
TIMES	Start time 10.59, end time 15.12, break at end of leg 00.50

If there is one animal I hate more than midges it is horseflies (known locally as clegs). As we start this section there are loads of them around, the amount I am sweating seems to be attracting them. Luckily, as long as I keep moving they are not biting, so it's a great motivation for me not to stop.

I enjoy this section over St Sunday Crag and Helvellyn. It's really hot but I think I must be getting used to it as I am moving well and picking up loads of time on my schedule, which I need to do as my stops are a lot longer than my planned ten minutes. As well as having Bill, Kim and Jane with me it is great that other people have also come out to see me, including family friend Mady Thompson, Gavin Bland and his wife Louise, and a couple of guys Al has found to do some filming. I am not looking forward to the long, 600-metre descent from Birkhouse Moor, but after some more codeine (a smaller dosage than the previous night …) I manage to run it all. I don't like taking painkillers when I run, but I feel this is a one-off and they will enable me to finish. As Kim says while we descend, it is only masking the pain. I manage to do the section in four hours and thirteen minutes instead of the scheduled five hours and fourteen minutes.

Mel: *'I followed my standard routine now. I would help get the trainers and socks off Steve, then give him a quick wash down with a sponge to remove sweat and dirt and to minimise chaffing. Then I would remove the dressings to see if any new areas were getting affected by blisters, hotspots or breaking down. Finally I would apply new dressings to cover the blisters. The dressings I used were Compeed, which is very useful for padding, followed by Mefix tape on top. Mefix is an elastic but thin dressing that doesn't add much volume in the shoe and shapes to the foot easily. It sticks well as long as feet are clean and dry. It is needed to hold Compeed secure as it is notorious for moving around when warm and wet and sticking like glue where you don't want it stuck, usually to socks as you pull them off quickly. To achieve dryness, after the initial use of talc, I worked on a prevention basis by liberally applying Bepanthen, a nappy rash cream, all over Steve's feet and between his toes. This also helped reduce friction between toes. Alcohol wipes were needed to help the Mefix stick in places, but required careful use due to exposed raw skin. I know this stung Steve's skin really badly but he was always very tolerant of what I did and never said a cross word to me. Only once asking politely "What did you use on my feet then? It really hurt", upon recovering from the shock. One of the big problems I had to deal with was the blisters on the lateral aspect of both of Steve's heels, just above the insole line, which were building up with pus. I lanced them at support points, and applied the Compeed on top (after liberally spraying with iodine), but they just kept filling up, and therefore causing pain. To deal with this I cut out the middle of the dressing and a middle section of the blister, then put a layer of Mefix over the top, thus providing some padding and protection while still allowing drainage.'*

SECTION 16   Glenridding Greenside Mine Road to Dockray, Sam Ware's House

DETAIL   23.2km, 1,270m ascent, 9 Wainwrights

SUPPORT TEAM   Nic Barber, Richard Suddaby and Andy Thompson

TIMES   Start time 16.02, end time 21.00, break at end of leg 00.53

I set off from the support point with Emma but without warning everyone else. So my support team have to run to catch me up. It is great to be joined by Nic, Richard and Andy again but my mind is going so I start asking Richard the same questions I did when he supported me on a section four days ago. The first top of the section is Glenridding Dodd, which I think is my final new Wainwright, although I cannot remember if I have been to the summit of Binsey, which I am due to go up at the end of day six.

It is now really hot, but the pace is fairly steady and it is not too humid, so it feels OK. David Bland, brother of Billy, is waiting to see us on White Side with some cool fresh spring water. I think I am running well as we contour back around Raise but David manages to walk in his big boots as fast as I can run. Maybe I am not moving that fast!

On the way up Great Dodd quite a few people come along and join us and with new faces, people to talk to and a big group I perk up a bit. One group that joins us is the O'Dowd family who I have never met before.

Ben and Gemma O'Dowd, aged twelve and ten years old: *'On Sunday 15 June Mum was watching the local news and saw an interview with Steve about his record attempt which he had started on the Saturday. On the Monday morning we found the link to the tracker that showed where he had been over the previous two days. Coincidentally, that same Sunday, we had had a damp day walking over two Wainwrights, Shipman Knotts and Kentmere Pike, and Gemma had asked what the record time was for completing the Wainwrights; the answer had been that we did not know – but it was probably Joss Naylor! We had just six Wainwrights*

THERE IS NO MAP IN HELL

left to complete ourselves. We wanted to support Steve, so looked at the tracker and decided to try to meet him on the Dodds, one of our favourite running grounds, on the Wednesday evening after school. As we came to the top of Great Dodd we could see a small group of people running towards Watson's Dodd. We were both excited and apprehensive as we ran off to meet them. Running off Great Dodd towards Clough Head seemed a quick descent for a man who had done five days of continuous running. We found running with Steve exhilarating and inspiring but he seemed to be delicate at times because of tiredness and his damaged feet. He even lay down and closed his eyes for a few minutes on the top of Clough Head. We tried to distract Steve from the hard hours ahead by talking to him about his family and our own mission to complete the Wainwrights.'

Clough Head is the last top on this section and seventy-five per cent of the way round – it is also directly above my house. As I descend from it I stop for a moment to look down and think how much I would like to be lying in bed at home. But instead I have a long tedious run along the Old Coach Road and then down the hill on a road to Dockray. I start by jogging slowly along the fairly flat Coach Road but eventually I slow down even more and it ends up as a fast walk. I say goodbye to the O'Dowd family at the end of the Coach Road and they say they will be out to see me finish. However, I still have doubts that I can finish this; I know there are two long hard days left, including a very long, tough section over the northern fells. If I can get through that section then the finish will be in sight.

In Dockray we have the use of the house of my running friends Sam Ware and Georgie Collinson. I go straight into their shower, which feels really refreshing. Afterwards I really enjoy the opportunity to sit in a comfy chair and eat pizza. It's really nice to see lots of people there and particularly to see my family, apart from James who is away on a school residential. It's three days since I have last seen Matthew and Hannah and it gives me a real lift mentally to see them again. For a while my self-centred thinking goes away and I can ask them questions about what has been happening to them and who has been looking after them. However, they can see and sense a complete change in me in the three days since I last saw them. Previously I looked tired but I was lively and happy, now I look completely drained. They can see the sparkle has gone. They cuddle me tightly while I eat and get treatment on my feet from Mel. But the treatment is really painful and it is hard to hide from them how sore it is. Although they do not say anything I can sense it is hard for them as well, but they know how much this means to me and they can see that sometimes it takes loads of effort to achieve the things you really want.

I spend an hour at the house (instead of the unrealistic ten minutes) so end up leaving thirty-one minutes down on schedule.

Shane wrote in the blog: *'Steve was much better mentally and more positive than when I saw him yesterday. The pain in his feet, legs and back, whilst significant, seems to have levelled out and he was focused on his goal and schedule. It is hard to really put your finger on the change but I felt that I was talking with someone whose mind was set and he was quietly confident that he would be successful. I think Steve has come to terms with the pain and has mental strategies for coping with it. That said, Steve is not looking forward to day six, as he knows that the Northern Fells are very rough underfoot and it is the rough terrain that is really slowing him down now. He knows that day six will be the crux of his Wainwright challenge and it is going to be a very tough and difficult day. Reflecting on Joss Naylor's record twenty-eight years ago, Steve knows that Joss's physical condition deteriorated very significantly in the last two days of the challenge. Obviously, Steve doesn't know whether this same fate awaits him or not. I guess he is a little nervous and certainly entering uncharted territory with the amount of abuse his body can take.'*

SECTION 17   Dockray, Sam Ware's House to Old A66 near Troutbeck
DETAIL   14km, 690m ascent, 3 Wainwrights
SUPPORT TEAM   Chris Baynham-Hughes, Jeff Powell Davies, Syd Coxen,
    Gary Baum and Sam Ware
TIMES   Start time 21.53, end time 00.25, break at end of leg 05.28

This is a short section with three small outlying fells. As usual with the smaller fells the navigation is quite tricky, especially as it is dusk as we set off. Luckily we have Sam with us who knows Gowbarrow really well as he lives so close and trains on it a lot. Later on we have Jeff who knew he was going to be doing this leg in the dark and so went out and reccied it a couple of days earlier.

As usual I really struggle to start moving again. Getting my muscles working and getting used to the blisters on my feet is really hard. I start off walking really slowly with both my family and a new support team of five people. After about five minutes my family turns back and eventually I start to speed up and make good progress. I reach the top of Gowbarrow having picked up a few minutes on the climb.

The descent from the final top of the section, Great Mell Fell, is really steep and grassy and suddenly the tendonitis, which has been sore for a couple of days, becomes agony. The angle of the slope seems to be perfect for irritating it and I am worried that this might cause me severe pain over the next two days. Eventually we reach the short road section to Troutbeck. It is nice to see family friends Steph and Dean Ratcliffe outside their house; they have come to say hello as I jog slowly past.

I am back on time when we reach the campervan parked at the edge of the old A66. I had originally thought about going home at this point and coming back to the same place the next morning. Joss did this on several nights but by this stage it just seems a waste of time. I know I am so tired that I will sleep well wherever I am.

I don't remember much about this stop, but Jim does some treatment on the muscles around my tendonitis then puts some tape on it and also gives me a general massage. Mel does more painful work on my blisters, which thankfully do not seem to be getting worse. As usual a massive variety of food, prepared by Emma and others, is offered to me. I eat well but a small fraction of what is available. I sleep well for four hours.

Mosedale Road End with the daunting prospect of a long section over the Northern Fells to come. Everything hurts but I remind myself that if I can finish this section, there is a good chance I can break the record. **Photo:** Steve Birkinshaw Collection.

23   DAY SIX

SECTION 18   Old A66 near Troutbeck to Mosedale Road End

DETAIL   13.8km, 890m ascent, 5 Wainwrights

SUPPORT TEAM   Chris Baynham-Hughes, Phil Davies, Andrew Davies and Andrew 'Scoffer' Schofield for part of the section

TIMES   Start time 05.53, end time 09.23, break at end of leg 00.39

This morning I am expecting the same as yesterday morning: agony to start with. I am not disappointed. I hobble down the road like a very old man. The footpaths across the fields are rough and painful; I walk the whole way. The guys try to lift my spirits but I am not happy. I eventually pick up a bit on the bracken-covered climb up to Souther Fell.

From here up to Blencathra the path is smooth and grassy and Scoffer appears, as he has a couple of hours before he needs to start work. Phil is in great spirits, and as we run past a partly decomposed sheep he films it and adds his own narration: 'Sorry Mr Sheep, but Steve was really hungry and needs must.' Then he turns the camera towards me: 'And there Steve goes with a belly full of mutton.' Scoffer can't be doing with this, and says to Phil, 'Stop arsing about and get an effing move on'. The two of them continue in this vein for the rest of the section, which helps to keep me amused.

Instead of my usual Torq gels that I have been eating while moving, I try to eat more normal food over the rest of the section but strangely it is making me feel really sick. I just about manage to keep it down but I cannot eat anything at the support point at the Mosedale road end. I just have some drink and let everything settle for a while. After leaving one hour and twenty-seven minutes down on my schedule at the start of this section I have actually picked up quite a bit of time to arrive only thirty-seven minutes down.

SECTION 19	Mosedale Road End to Dodd Wood Car Park
DETAIL	37.5km, 2,200m ascent, 17 Wainwrights
SUPPORT TEAM	Martin Indge, Chris Baynham-Hughes, Jim Mann, Paul 'Corny' Cornforth and Nic Davies
TIMES	Start time 10.02, end time 19.35, break at end of leg 01.08

This is a crucial ten-hour section over the northern fells. But cleverly my support team decide to split it into two with an additional stop above Whitewater Dash. This is about an hour's walk uphill from the nearest road, so it is great they are happy to do it as it makes the section much easier mentally.

Emma: *'I have the day off work and the children are at school so I finally have the chance to run with Steve; it is lovely to get up Carrock Fell and I am encouraged to see how well Steve is running once he gets warmed up. Maybe there is a chance he can complete it now. I would love to run further, but I have a long shopping list of things to buy including Torq gels (about all he is eating whilst running now), cream and dressings for his feet. I also have a heap of sweaty running clothes to wash and food to cook.'*

It is really nice that Emma has time to join me up Carrock Fell. She has been incredibly busy sorting out everything, so the fact she has managed to get an hour and a half on the fells with me is great. It also gives her a chance to see me when I am going well and happy out on the fells rather than at the support points when I am at my worst.

As we go along this section it begins to dawn on me how many people are interested in my progress. I was expecting some interest amongst the fell-running community, but the interest is much wider than I ever imagined and growing rapidly. The mixture of the trackers, the regular blogs, television and social media mean that thousands of people are now really excited about my progress. As well as people watching my progress from their computer screens, they are also coming out to see me. So when we arrive on High Pike someone comes up and gives a generous donation. Then some fell runners who I recognise but do not know turn up. These are Paul Dobson, Andrew Martindale, and Paul and Chris Wilson, and they run with us for a couple of hours. From the top of Brae Fell I can see the next top, Longlands Fell, and there is a massive flag on top. It seems a bit strange and we all wonder why someone would have done that. When we get there we find that it has been put up for *me* by Jeff Ford, who lives locally and is chair of the Mountain Heritage Trust. I had never met Jeff before, but like so many other people he had been following my progress and came out to give me some support.

My afternoon dip happens as we approach Great Cockup. I suddenly come over extremely sleepy; I am walking along barely able to keep my eyes open. The guys try pouring water over my head and talking to me but it is no use. I need to sleep. So, on the top of Great Cockup I decide

I *have* to have a power nap. I lie down with a rucksack as a pillow and close my eyes. Meanwhile Jim Mann decides to fill in the time by running around with the tracker so it will make a picture on the OS map that thousands of people are following on the Open Tracking website. After five minutes I suddenly get up and start moving again – unfortunately Jim does not have time to finish his picture. I feel slightly less sleepy but for the next hour I am still really struggling to stay awake. I feel like I am midway between being awake and asleep.

The descent off Little Calva to the track above Whitewater Dash is heathery without any real path. I place my foot badly on many occasions and let out a little scream as the shoes press on my blister. I am desperate to get through this descent but I am even more worried about the descent from Ullock Pike at the end of this section, which is even rougher with taller heather and no path at all. It is good to finally reach the track and see the support team of Jon Bardgett and Mel and Kate Culleton-Wright. I have food, drink and more foot treatment and another little doze.

The big climb up Skiddaw goes well and at the summit there are more people looking out for me, together with Al Lee and Rob Jarman doing some filming. After all the difficulties of the first two days it is great that Al and Rob have finally caught up with me when the tops of the fells are clear of cloud. After Skiddaw there is a long out-and-back to Lonscale Fell and as we approach this top Andy Blackett turns up with some ice creams. He has carried them up from Keswick in an ice bag – a really nice surprise. The ice cream goes down very well on such a nice warm afternoon, although with my lack of coordination a lot of it ends up on my face.

As we approach Ullock Pike I have a discussion with Scoffer, who has turned up after work, and Corny about the route down that I am dreading. We decide it will be better to go back over Long Side, contour round Carl Side and then down the path, which is a bit longer than my planned route but avoids the knee-deep heather. I can run the descent, so it's a good route. There are even more people on the top of Dodd, the last top in this section. I was planning on taking the north-west ridge off Dodd but again we make a sensible decision and decide to take the longer route which goes along a good track. I descend well running at nine-minute-mile pace according to Bill Williamson's GPS.

There are around twenty people waiting for me as we get to Dodd Wood car park, including Emma, Matthew and Hannah. I arrive there one minute up on my schedule, although as usual I will leave quite a bit behind due to my longer-than-anticipated stops. We follow the normal routine of getting washed and straight in the campervan. Eating is getting progressively harder; anything even slightly warm feels really painful as it goes down my throat. Tepid soup seems to be best at the moment. I don't know what Mel is doing to my feet but it is absolute *agony* – the worst yet. With Matthew and Hannah present I try really hard not to scream out in pain and show them how terrible it is, but I cannot help a few squeaks. Eventually, it is so painful I grab a towel to muffle the sound and so that they cannot see the tears in my eyes from the pain. Matthew is really sweet and gives me a hug and says 'it will be worth it when you have finished'.

I know my body is gradually disintegrating. Everything is becoming harder and slower. My mind is gradually going and all I can focus on is just moving forward – one foot in front of the other. I do not even try to think about anything else, that is what my support team is for, and they do everything brilliantly. Talking is sometimes hard, so if I no longer need my poles I just throw them down as I know someone will pick them up for me. Luckily the end is almost within reach and it is approaching a bit faster than the rate at which my body is falling apart. But it is a close-run thing.

Shane writes on the blog: *'I chatted with Steve at Dodd Wood whilst nurse Mel tortured his feet. I think it would be fair to say that Steve's discomfort and pain whilst moving has levelled off but his speed has dropped. He is clearly knackered in a deep and fundamental way to such an extent that at times he is disconnecting from the conversation surrounding him and drifting off into semi-conscious waking. Just as quickly he will snap back to the reality of the situation, often when nurse Mel inflicts some pain! We talked about the surge of adrenaline tomorrow will bring, knowing that if he just walks to Keswick, he will almost certainly break the record.*

A few people have asked whether they can run the last section with Steve. I've checked with Steve and he is very happy for runners to join him. The more the merrier! If you are keen to run with Steve this will be a once-in-a-generation opportunity to see a major fell-running record broken (fingers crossed everything still goes to plan). Regardless, it would be fantastic for Steve to have a big crowd of runners to accompany him on the last section or see him finish in Keswick. If he is on schedule it'll mean leaving Newland Hause at roughly 18.00 on Friday evening and running (slowly)/walking to Keswick. It is seventeen kilometres with 1,000 metres of ascent. Steve should arrive in Keswick at about 23.00. Anyone joining Steve will need to check his tracker to make sure they arrive at Newlands Hause in time to join him as obviously his timings may change. I'll keep the blog as up to date as I can with the ETA.'

SECTION 20	Dodd Wood Car Park to Pheasant Inn
DETAIL	17.5km, 430m, 1 Wainwright
SUPPORT TEAM	Lee Newton, Bill Stewart and Morgan Donnelly, with Gavin Bland and Jon Bardgett on bikes
TIMES	Start time 20.43, end time 23.25, break at end of leg 06.05

When I worked out my route this was the only section that I was dreading doing as eighty per cent of it is on roads with a small climb up to the only Wainwright on the section – Binsey. However, at Dodd Wood at the end of the previous section I am actually hoping it might be better than the rest of the day, as the smooth surface means no twisting of my foot and so the blisters will not be very sore. I am also hoping that changing shoes to my Berghaus Vapour Claws will help. However, as soon as I set off I realise just how tired I am, and even without pain from my blisters I am moving very slowly and the pounding from the hard road surface makes my legs very sore. I just about manage a gentle jog on the road to Bassenthwaite village but it is frustratingly slow for Morgan (British fell-running champion), Bill and Lee who are running, while Gavin and Jon are on their bikes and struggling not to fall off as the speed is so slow.

Just as we approach Bassenthwaite village I become desperate for a poo but it is hard to find a suitable spot in the village. Luckily there is a pub so I quickly run in there. On the way out I notice England are playing their second football match in the world cup and are losing again, this time to Uruguay.

The uphill road section, before the final climb up a track to the summit of Binsey, is a relief as I have a good excuse to walk. Soon after in the dusk I am walking up the final climb to the summit, and it is actually quite enjoyable as there is a beautiful view over the Solway Estuary. It is great to see Jeff Ford with his England flag again and also my friend, Claire Smits. With other friends, Ben Bardsley, Angie Turnbull and Mady Thompson joining us there is quite a big group for the descent to the

Castle Inn. I am desperate to run along the flat road section to the next support point at the Pheasant Inn, as if I do I can pick up a lot of time on my schedule. It is less than two kilometres but I just cannot manage to run it and I settle for a fast walk. The last ten minutes are desperate as I am half asleep and just want to stop and fall asleep at the side of the road. But I make it to the campervan.

> **Emma:** *'Steve arrived in better spirits than I have seen for several days; he has survived the road run to Binsey, thanks to lots of good support. But his body is falling apart; can he hold it together for one more day? I sort his stuff out, although I am a bit useless and cannot find some of the food. I get some film of Steve rambling incoherently.'*

Celebrating my completion of the Wainwrights on the Moot Hall steps with Jane Saul, who sorted out all the logistics. Photo Mike Pearson.

24   DAY SEVEN

SECTION 21   Pheasant Inn to Whinlatter Hobcarton Car Park

DETAIL   14.8km, 1,070m ascent, 7 Wainwrights

SUPPORT TEAM   Howard Seal, Lee Newton, Nick Ray, Graham Watson, Nina Walkinshaw, Jim Davies and Andrew Davies

TIMES   Start time 05.30, end time 08.58, break at end of leg 00.55

The thought of another long day out running on painful blisters is too much for me and I start to cry. I have managed to stay tough for six days but I have reached the limit of what I can take. After a bit of a discussion we decide to cut holes in a couple of pairs of shoes to give my feet space to expand and reduce the pressure on my blisters. Jim Davies comes into the campervan to show us what to do. Jim has a massive bunion on each foot so he has become an expert at cutting bits out of his shoes. After about forty minutes and lots of trial and error we have four carefully cut shoes. There are now holes around the little toes and also on the outside of the heels. However, this does mean we leave two hours and eleven minutes behind schedule.

Nick Ray knows these hills very well and leads the way, taking us up the nice track route to Sale Fell. The holes in my shoes give me instant relief and after a good rest I am really moving well again. The flat, rough, boggy land after Ling Fell is still uncomfortable but we are soon back on the nice short grassy terrain. I am in a good mood and my mental low from the morning is gone, I finally know I can do this and the end does seem to be in sight. I start counting down the tops. Ling Fell is number 188, so only twenty-six to go.

We are not sure which of the three Graystones summits is the Wainwright and so we end up visiting them all. We do know which the Wainwright is for Whinlatter fell and unfortunately it is another kilometre past the highest point. This is a pain but that is what Wainwright chose so we must go there. The straight-line descent off here is really rough – there is no path just a mixture of deep heather and loose rocks – so we take a longer route avoiding the worst of the rocks, which allows me to do some bum shuffling down the hill with waterproof trousers on. Although I still have to walk across some bits with rocks, which is really painful. This is the final pathless descent of the entire run, and I know I can cope with rocky or grassy descents. This makes me feel happy as I wander into the Hobcarton car park to meet my support crew. I have picked up one hour and ten minutes on this section.

Shane writes on the blog: *'Steve explained to me that his feet were so sore now that he was literally screaming in pain when his footfall wasn't perfect. As if on cue, a dog began howling outside and Steve said, "Yes, just like that, but imagine someone was standing on his tail at the same time." Steve enjoyed a nice continental breakfast including croissant and fresh fruit. He is drinking a mixture of Torq energy drink and water on the fells and is staying hydrated enough to keeping weeing, which is one of the first questions his medics are asking at each stop. For pain management Steve is mixing a concoction of different painkillers and the medics and support runners are keeping a careful note of what and when he is taking them. To illustrate the point, yesterday evening Steve asked for some more Ibuprofen and said he "hadn't had any for hours and hours". We checked with his support runners and they said he'd had some less than an hour ago!'*

SECTION 22	Whinlatter Hobcarton Car Park to Rannerdale Car Park
DETAIL	9.3km, 630m ascent, 3 Wainwrights
SUPPORT TEAM	Paul Hainsworth, Sam Ware, Nick Ray, John Kewley and Nic Davies
TIMES	Start time 09.53, end time 12.10, break at end of leg 00.55

When I planned this section I was worried about the big climb up the first Wainwright of the section – Grisedale Pike. But once I start the climb I feel good and I am climbing at fifteen metres per minute again. If I ever begin to feel slightly tired I take a Torq gel and five minutes later I perk up. Although my body seems to be disintegrating it also seems to have adapted. Any energy I put in goes straight to where it is needed. So the scheduled one hour and twenty-five minutes to the top of Grisedale Pike only takes fifty-one minutes; again I have picked up lots of time after my slower-than-scheduled stop. The run along the ridge past Hopegill Head to Whiteside is really enjoyable. I change my shoes for the long descent to Rannerdale; the Vapour Claws with the holes in are really comfortable but too loose for a steep rocky descent so I put on my X-Talons and make good progress down to the road.

Emma is unable to make this support point so Jon Bardgett takes over her duties – including giving me a big hug! Mel is now happy my feet will not get any worse before the finish so only does a little bit of work on them. I am just about ready to go but suddenly I feel sleepy. I know I can now do this but I still have thirty-seven kilometres and 1,690 metres of climbing to go before the finish. So nearly a marathon distance-wise and two times up and down Scafell Pike from Wasdale Head climbing-wise. They are still big numbers, and I do not want to be walking half asleep zombie-like for a couple of hours like yesterday. So I go for a proper power nap. I get into the campervan and have thirty minutes' sleep – leaving everyone outside sitting patiently in the sun for me to finish my sleep and be ready to go. I hope this will get me to the finish without needing any more sleep. I leave one hour and fifty minutes behind schedule, but I know I can pick most of this up.

> **Shane writes on the blog:** *'It is clear that Steve's general health is now suffering. This is no longer about sore feet and tired legs but total systemic body exhaustion. After sucking on his asthma inhaler, Steve has a productive chesty cough that might keep some people off work for the day! When you glance at Steve sometimes he looks just a little jaded, but on other occasions you can see a deeply drawn expression on his face that only comes with extreme fatigue.'*

SECTION 23	Rannerdale Car Park to Newlands Hause
DETAIL	19.8km, 1,670m ascent, 12 Wainwrights
SUPPORT TEAM	Craig Smith, Andy Slattery, Sam Ware, Howard Leslie, Vicky Ware and Lewis Taylor. Marcus Byron for part of the section, and loads more towards the end of the section
TIMES	Start time 13.05, end time 18.03, break at end of leg 00.18

The battle for the person to do the most number of Wainwrights with me has intensified. Nic Barber turns up to take his total over the week to fifty-five, but we think Mark Roberts and Corny will appear at some point in the day. But when and how many will they do with me?

Rannerdale Knotts is a short steep climb before the long drag up Whiteless Pike. As usual I make good progress up the climb and pick up time on my schedule. My knee is stiffening up badly as we approach Grasmoor; Marcus gives me a quick massage on the muscles around it which seems to help.

I forgot to put any sun cream on at Rannerdale and as I have taken my shirt off again I am worried about my shoulders burning. None of the guys have any with them but someone asks a passing walker who luckily has some. Howard suggests a change of plan on the four Wainwrights which form a loop from the col between Sail and Scar Crags and I agree that it makes sense to do it anticlockwise and take Causey Pike before Barrow as overall the running is better.

As we approach Barrow it is around 5 p.m. on Friday evening and loads of people have finished work and start to appear. It's amazing that they are all here just to run with me. Mark Roberts joins me on Barrow and Corny on Ard Crags and they work out that if they stay with me to the end then Mark will win the competition of most Wainwrights with me with fifty-six, followed by Nic with fifty-five and Corny fifty-three. With all the people around I start to go really well, and there must be fifty people running with me as I descend towards Newlands Hause. My family have walked up a bit from Newlands Hause and run back down with me. James, who is just back from four days away at his school residential, looks astonished to see more and more runners appear. There are even more people waiting for me in the car park at Newlands Hause and I get a big cheer as I come in and sit down. Amazingly I have picked up one hour and fifty-five minutes on my schedule for this section and I arrive five minutes up. There is no point in doing anything with my feet, they will get me to the finish now. The children and Emma give me hugs. Matthew asks me which is my favourite Wainwright and I reply, 'The last one!'

Emma: *'It is amazing to see so many people here. James, Matthew and Hannah are delighted to see Steve and stay close to him all the time. On the first day I told them this was going to be a strange week, but a once-in-a-lifetime experience, so they should make the most of it. Little did I realise how true that would be. It has been hard for them too, and I worry it may have put them off doing any running ever, but they have shown such empathy, hugging Steve when in pain and saying "don't worry, you'll be finished soon".'*

Kim Baxter, who has come especially from Sheffield, gives my legs a quick massage.

Kim: *'During Steve's six days of running I became very obsessed with following his progress on the GPS tracker. For that week, time, or more accurately gaps in time became measured in Wainwrights, I got the kids to school – a Wainwright was eaten, I saw a patient, and returned to see more Wainwrights gobbled up. Bedtime was delayed to ensure the little dot continued to move, and my first task when waking was to check on progress. On the final day of the challenge with Steve on course to break the record I did my only spontaneous act since having children and raced from Sheffield to Newlands Hause to share the final leg with Steve and many others.'*

I manage to eat a bit of food and, just before I go, Jon Bardgett gets everyone around and gives a rousing speech. He speaks about what an amazing achievement this is, and thanks everyone for coming along and supporting me. It's really nice of him, although I am slightly embarrassed by all the fuss … I have no idea what is awaiting me in Keswick.

I leave after only eighteen minutes. I know I am going to complete this in a new record and I know I will be up on my schedule by the time I finish. I only have four hours or so until the finish and I already feel quite emotional.

Shane writes in the blog: *'At this support point Steve was in a great mood and clearly delighted with the number of support runners that had turned out. He said, "My blisters aren't so sore anymore and I'm getting a real boost running with friends and so many other well-wishers".'*

SECTION 24	Newlands Hause to Keswick Moot Hall
DETAIL	17.2km, 1,020m ascent, 6 Wainwrights
SUPPORT TEAM	Paul 'Corny' Cornforth, Mark Roberts, Peter Murphy, Ryan Wood, Ben Thompson and loads of others
TIMES	Start time 18.21, end time 22.01

With around fifty people I start the climb up Robinson and the last six Wainwrights. I feel a bit like Forrest Gump in the scene where he sets off across the country collecting a band of followers. However, as much as I am trying to run fast everyone is running away from me!

Al Lee: *'During the day I organised a helicopter and arranged to meet the pilot at Gavin Bland's farm near Thirlmere. The weather was absolutely perfect – great light, no wind and warm. The lack of wind was important as I didn't have a stabiliser organised for the camera. I was just clipped in and filmed out of the open door with Rob Jarman in charge of passing me the correct camera. Unfortunately our timing was not right and Steve was sitting down on a deck chair at Newlands Hause when we flew over. I desperately hoped he was going to have a short break as the helicopter only had an hour and a half of fuel. Whilst waiting the pilot flew over the Langdale Pikes and Scafell so I got some stunning shots of these for the film. Then when we returned to Steve he was climbing and then descending from Robinson with the large group of supporters running with him, and the footage I got was perfect. We returned to Gavin's farm and then drove to Keswick and I got set up at the top of the steps of the Moot Hall ready to capture Steve's finish.'*

The legendary Billy Bland who holds the thirteen hours and fifty-three-minute record for the Bob Graham Round turns up as we approach Dale Head. It is great to have a quick chat with him and a shake of his hand. Chris Knox, who helped Joss on his round, also runs with me on this section and it is interesting to hear from him how much of a bad way Joss was in as he approached the finish.

Eventually my final top, Wainwright number 214, Cat Bells, is in sight. Everyone else has overtaken me and is waiting as I approach it. I get a massive round of applause as I walk slowly up to the top. Jane is there and gives me a big hug and hands me a bottle of Wainwright beer. I have a few sips and although it would be nice to finish the bottle and enjoy the view I need to continue, as the run is only complete when I get back to my starting point at Keswick Moot Hall.

Ben and Gemma O'Dowd: *'After seeing Steve on day five we avidly followed his progress in the following days, checking the tracker against his predicted times before and after school and reading the blog. We worried for him if he got behind time and considered possible reasons, whilst there was relief when he made time back up or got ahead. The live tracker was brilliant. We wanted to join Steve again to witness this fantastic record so we went up to Newlands Pass to run up Robinson with him. We were slightly earlier than Steve's expected arrival time so jogged up towards Knott Rigg where he would be coming from. Halfway up we heard a huge cheer and we realised that he had already reached the pass and we were heading in the opposite direction so we turned around and ran hard to catch the crowd of well-wishers surrounding Steve. After getting to the top of Robinson we returned to the van parked at Newlands Pass and drove to the base of Cat Bells. After a short rest and sort out, we set off briskly for the top, arriving as Steve took his first sip of beer. Throngs of people surrounded him and there was a jubilant atmosphere. Steve's mood on Cat Bells was a complete contrast to when we saw him on day five; he appeared to be excited and relieved that the pressure was removed from him as he was nearing the completion of his dream. We headed off with him and the rest of the crowd towards Keswick. We have been inspired by his achievement and were amazed by how fast he completed the Wainwrights considering we took ten years. Putting this into perspective, he did them about 500 times quicker than us. We both continue to enjoy running and are spurred on by Steve's achievements. Gemma has a map with Steve's route marked up on her bedroom wall in preparation for her future attempt for the record! It was great to witness and to play a small part in this incredible achievement.'*

All I need to do is get off Cat Bells safely but the descent is very steep and rocky to start with. Normally I can run down, jumping easily from rock to rock. But not surprisingly after six and a half days I am a bit wobbly on my feet so I take it carefully using my poles for support. As we approach the bottom of the rocky bit, an older man who has come out to see me several times during the week and has run with me from Barrow, trips up and rolls into me, breaking his glasses. With the help of my poles I just manage to keep my balance so neither of us end up rolling down the hill towards Derwent Water. We are both OK but Corny shouts 'Has Joss sent you to sabotage this attempt?!'

I feel tired but keep up a slow run all the way to Portinscale, less than two kilometres from the finish. However, in Portinscale I am suddenly desperate for a poo. What do I do? I don't want to rush into the bushes as we approach the Moot Hall or even worse need to go while standing on the steps of the Moot Hall. Luckily Corny has some friends in the village; he knocks on their door and then shouts through the letter box. They let us in, and I am literally very relieved. However, the fifty or so people running with me have absolutely no idea what is going on and are standing in the street wondering where I am and when I will start running again.

It is hard to put into words the emotions I feel as I run up to the Moot Hall. For six and a half days I have pushed hard, I have been sick, had massive open blisters on my feet and tendonitis in my leg. I have been so exhausted that I have been falling asleep as I have been walking. Sometimes it has felt like a hell that was never going to finish. Until the last day I never even knew if I could succeed. But I have carried on and on, pushing myself harder and further than I have ever done before. Further than I ever thought I could. I know I am now very near my limit but I have made it. I have completed all the Wainwrights in six days and thirteen hours and I have a new record. Unbelievably, I have beaten the legendary Joss Naylor by over twelve hours.

Emma: *'The original plan in my mind was for me and the children to run the very last part with Steve, but he's going so well there is no way we would be able to keep up with him and James is shattered having just finished his school residential in Coniston. We head for Keswick and the Moot Hall; there are literally hundreds of people around which seems a bit strange for this time of night. What is happening? There are friends and neighbours we recognise there but also a lot of other people, and it turns out they have all come to see Steve finish! I had envisaged just a few people, this is unbelievable! The children find some of their friends and play Tig around the Moot Hall and so are happy. Al Lee is there filming from the steps, and Mike Pearson is taking stills and we are told we should head up there to meet Steve. All our children's friends think it looks like fun and come up too, hence on some of the photos it looks as if we have eight children! An advance runner comes in to announce Steve is on his way, and then we see him, running through the crowds at a good pace. Tears come to my eyes; he's definitely going to finish it! The happiness and relief is indescribable, he is completely broken but has actually, after nearly a week of running, succeeded.'*

As well as the fifty people running with me there are a couple of hundred waiting around the Moot Hall. A massive cheer goes up as I get in sight, then a huge wall of noise gets louder and louder as I approach. A gap opens up through the crowds and there I am at the bottom of the Moot Hall steps. I climb the steps and touch the door to confirm my finish. I am congratulated and hugged by Emma then James, Matthew, Hannah and my mum. I am so happy to have achieved my aim but also completely overwhelmed with exhaustion. There are some tears, but I try not to cry too much. The cheering and clapping lasts for ages. It is an incredible feeling and the end of the most amazing day and week of my life. Then just as the noise drops a bit, Hannah gives me a medal she has made, which is a chocolate coin with a nice ribbon, and as I put it on the clapping intensifies again.

> **Al Lee:** *'The first few days filming were a nightmare. But seeing Steve finish in Keswick on the last day was one of the most inspiring and uplifting things I have witnessed. The atmosphere in Keswick that night was simply amazing.'*

Fell running is generally a solitary sport. I do not run for fame or fortune but because I enjoy being outside in all weathers on the fells. I do not crave or even particularly like the spotlight, but here I am – the centre of attention. My efforts have obviously inspired a lot of people and I am so grateful they have made the effort to come out and see me. If my achievement encourages more people to get out and enjoy the fells that is great. I hope it will make them as happy as it makes me.

After the amazing cheering died down I walked down the steps of the Moot Hall and sat on the bottom step with a pint of Wainwright beer in my hand. There was a long line of people who came up to shake my hand. Many of these people had supported me on the way round, and I will always be grateful to them for the help they gave me. I was so happy and would have loved to have stood around chatting but I was also absolutely exhausted and it was time for some rest and recovery.

Emma drove me home, I had a quick shower and went to sleep in my own bed. The doctors also gave me a couple of sleeping pills to make sure I did sleep and recover. I have never taken sleeping pills before and I took one and slept quite well, although my legs were quite twitchy as if they were still expecting to be moving the whole time. Four hours later I took the other tablet and got another good sleep.

The next day I could just about hobble around the house but all my joints ached and I was still struggling mentally – talking in coherent sentences was very hard. After breakfast, then another sleep and lunch, I needed to write something on my blog as I knew thousands of people were interested. I am a slow writer at the best of times, but it took me over an hour to get my thoughts together and be able to type the following sentences all filled with spelling mistakes and grammatical errors:

> This has been the most amazing week of my life. At times it was so painful and I have felt like giving up. But the reception I received in Keswick make it all worthwhile. I am finding it hard to write and put everything into words. I get quite emotionally thinking about the entire journey. I would like to thank at team of around 100 people who have helped me in various ways during the week, without whom what I have achieved would have been impossible. So thank you everyone. I will write a proper thank you in my next blog. Last night and today I have been sleeping and eating. Sleeping has been helped by some painkillers to relieve the pain but it has still been a bit fitfull. I can hobble around the house very slowly. Everything is very swollen and it was quite a scary sight looking at my myself in the mirror for the first time in seven days. Thanks everyone who has turned my dream into a reality.

Despite a similarly small amount of sleep, Emma wrote the following in a couple of minutes:

> *'I'd like to finish by saying thank you to everyone, this really was a team effort, there are so many of you I don't want to mention names in case I forget anyone, but you know who you are. To everyone who supported Steve or me in any way, thank you for making this happen. I'd like to finish by quoting from the legendary Joss Naylor's account of his Wainwrights round. While many things have changed in twenty-eight years, some things remain the same. "To find words to express my gratitude to those who took part is beyond me … It will be a very lucky man who is able to make the bonds of friendship which have been my good luck. To all my 'team' thank you from the bottom of my heart".'*

The rest of that day and the following day are a bit of a blur. All I remember is that I ate a lot and when I was not eating I lay on the sofa groaning or sometimes I just went back to bed. Emma was amazing as ever and carried on looking after me and the children and sorting out a press release with the Berghaus guys, even though she needed sleep as much as me. However, there was still lots to sort out. There was kit and spare food all over the house, lots of the media were interested in my story and there was also the social media to deal with.

> **Jane:** *'The whole week was really exciting, with loads of giggles but also incredibly hard. I had a very long drive around the Lake District and caught up with my Lakes mates but I did not have time to stop in one cafe or pub. My food consisted of leftovers once Steve and his hill-support team had eaten everything they wanted. At night the road-support team were surviving on about two hours' sleep (our first priority was sorting out getting Steve to sleep, then tidying up, before waking up early to make Steve porridge and sorting out maps and Steve's kit*

for the next support runners). There was little time to get washed and I managed just one shower in the week. The whole support team were great and despite frequent changes of plan and being tired there was never a cross word said. After Steve had finished I was so tired I could not talk; I needed to go somewhere to relax and recover. Jon Bardgett and Nic Davies looked after me and took me away in the campervan to a quiet spot. Then next day after a swim in Derwent Water they took me back to their house for some more quiet recovery time.'

Two local television news crews came round to our house on the third day after I finished. I just about managed to hobble up and down the drive in my Vapour Claws with holes cut into them. I answered lots of emails but I was still struggling mentally and as a result I was typing at a snail's pace. Actually, it was worse than that. I was typing slowly but the words in my brain did not come out correctly when I typed so I would have to go back and correct nearly every word.

I still had a lot of recovering to do.

4 The Aftermath

25 THE PHYSICAL AND MENTAL IMPACT

After the elation of the first three days after I had finished, the post-run blues hit me really badly. Firstly, I had my worst ever headache. I sometimes get migraine-type headaches but this was several levels worse. Every time I moved it felt like my head was going to explode. Even lying down still it was very sore. After a day, this began to gradually ease but then I started to have negative thoughts about my completion of the Wainwrights and the new record. Instead of being delighted to have done it I started thinking about all the time I spent not moving while having my feet sorted and how I should have managed a much faster time. I almost felt like a fraud that everyone thought I had done so brilliantly. I was expecting the blues a bit from my experiences of previous long runs and also from having talked to other people who had done similar things, but it was worse than I was expecting. After a couple more days my mood improved and I again appreciated the enormous achievement of my run.

The negative thoughts I experienced after I finished were nothing compared to how much Joss suffered. In the audiocassette tape Joss recorded once he had returned home he says: 'The worst part was still to come. For the next five nights I ran the last section of the Wainwrights four times. From the moment I lay down and went to sleep, I ran until I wakened. I wakened in a pool of sweat and this happened for five consecutive nights. I went down to practically eight stone … It makes you realise when you do these things that you have to be prepared mentally and physically or you can end up in a state where you need psychiatric treatment.' For someone as tough and strong as Joss to suffer so much afterwards highlights how hard this challenge is and how much it can take out of you.

A lot of people commented when I finished that I was looking much thinner in my face and my body – although there was also quite a lot of swelling around my eyes – so when I weighed myself I was expecting a significant loss in weight. However, I was exactly the same weight as before I started. The reason was that although I had lost a lot of fat, my legs and feet were all puffed up and swollen with lots of excess fluid having been retained, and these losses and gains balanced each other out. The fluid in my legs and feet took a couple of weeks to completely go and by then I had eaten so much food I was still the same weight. While the swelling in my feet and legs was going down a layer of skin was also falling off my feet and my blisters were recovering. This meant that two weeks after I had finished my feet had recovered really well – all the hard dead skin had fallen off and been replaced by nice soft skin. So, apart from my toenails, they actually looked loads better than before I started. The horrible-looking toenails were actually not due to my Wainwrights run but due to many years of abuse from fell running and orienteering. Apart from the one good toenail (the middle toe on my left foot) all the rest had fallen off or were black before I started.

I tried to go back to work in Newcastle six days after I had finished. It was great to see my work colleagues and loads of them had been reading my blog and following my progress on the tracker. However, my attempts at work were useless. It was obvious to everyone that I was still completely 'spaced out' and unable to concentrate. I was virtually told not to bother doing any work, and to just go home, relax and recover. I was actually quite surprised as I thought I would be mentally quite alert after three or four days.

26 REFLECTING ON MY WAINWRIGHTS RUN

While I was recovering I had the chance to think about my seven days running round the Wainwrights and whether or not I enjoyed it. Running into Keswick on the seventh day with hundreds of people cheering and my family waiting for me was an amazing and special feeling. It was definitely the best running day of my life. But how about the rest of it? I obviously suffered a lot during those seven days so you would have thought the answer was no, I could not have enjoyed it. However, one of the things I enjoy most in my life is running and walking on the Lake District fells. So I think the answer is that I can enjoy something even if it is hurting at the same time. I can enjoy the view from a summit and running along a ridge even with blisters on my feet that make each step agony. I know I could not have put up with that amount of pain and suffering if I had been running round a city. The other key to my enjoyment was having at least two friends with me the whole time. Having them there being supportive, friendly, happy and encouraging made such a positive impact. On only three occasions was I slightly annoyed by anyone and these were when someone was doing their best but it was not quite the right thing at the right time. I never said anything at the time and never will, as these people are true friends and had made an effort and given their time to help me.

What would Alfred Wainwright himself have made of my run? In his book *Fellwalking with Wainwright*, he writes of the Fairfield Horseshoe, 'Fellrunners will complete the whole round in less than two hours without seeing anything other than the track before them. I admire those who can perform such feats. I envy their fitness but not their achievements; racers and record breakers seem to me to be out of place on the high fells. Mountains are there to be enjoyed, and enjoyed leisurely. I could never have travelled at speed on foot, nor have I ever wanted to. Sour grapes don't enter into it. My preference is to walk slowly, halting often to look around and see what is to be seen.'

It is a shame that he would not have approved but I think it is due to a misunderstanding of fell runners. As other fell runners have noted, just because we are running does not mean we are not enjoying being in the fells. For example, Alan Heaton wrote, 'Sometimes people wonder if fell runners ever stop and stare. They may not stop very much but they do stare'. Personally I love being in the fells. I love being up high looking at the view and feeling the wind on my face. I enjoy moving fast but I will often stop on a summit and look around. I do not just look at the track in front of me – except when I am descending in a race – I look around seeing how the clouds are moving and the fells are chang- ing in the different light. Like Alfred Wainwright and Joss Naylor, I have a love of the fells, which is why I live in the Lake District and get out at every opportunity.

One of the things I found most strange on my run was how close I stayed to my schedule. I was almost always within two hours of it. The way I worked it out was not very scientific but it obviously turned out to be accurate. At the end I was still climbing well and a lot faster than the eight metres per minute in the schedule, so I was picking up lots of time on these climbs. On the grassy descents I was staying just about level with the schedule. On the steep rocky descents I was losing quite a bit of time, for example on the West Wall Traverse down from Scafell to Lingmell I lost about twenty minutes. The biggest difference from the schedule was that I needed lots of treatment on my feet, so from the third day onwards I was often spending around an hour at the end of a section – which was not completely wasted time as I was also eating and drinking well in that hour – whereas on the schedule these stops were only meant to be ten minutes. I also failed to sleep on the first couple of nights so from then onwards I gave myself an extra hour at night. So the final approximate totals are (with Joss's in brackets):

Total time: 157 hours (*169 hours*)
Resting time: 42 hours (*44 hours*)
Moving time: 115 hours (*125 hours*)

What is interesting about this, is that when I was moving I was clearly moving well. The route is basically five Bob Graham Rounds, so when I was moving, I was on average slightly faster than a twenty-four-hour Bob Graham Round pace. I was also, on average, moving faster than Joss. At the start I was slower than him, but my speed dropped off less than Joss's so by the end I was moving considerably faster.

My feeling is that I was over ambitious in how fast I could do a transition between two sections, but if I had not needed treatment on my feet I could have saved a lot of time. However, it does make me think there is potential to improve on the record. If someone can move at the speed I did but manage to avoid any blisters or injuries – not easy – they could reduce the resting time and break the record.

27 GETTING BACK TO NORMAL

After three weeks I felt ready to start running again. My first couple of runs were short and very slow. They were very slow partly out of choice but also because I could not run any faster. I was really struggling to breathe even on the flat and the slightest hill was a massive effort to run up. I was expecting this but not to quite such an extent. The good thing was that my legs felt OK. The muscles seemed in really good condition, mainly thanks to the regular massages I'd received from Jim and Phil Davies during the Wainwrights.

In order to gauge how slowly I was running I tried my regular timed run. This consists of two intervals up a hill along a good path. My cumulative best time for these two is six minutes and fifty seconds. This time I did it in eight minutes and five seconds. I was surprised how much slower I was. What I was not sure about was if this reduced speed was because I needed more recovery time or the opposite – it was six weeks since I had done my last really fast run, two weeks before the Wainwrights, and my body was just not used to running fast. I thought it was probably a combination of the two. So I decided to carry on running and training but not to do really hard weeks.

A week later my timed run was down to seven minutes and thirty-five seconds, so I was making progress. I felt up to doing a fell race, so I ran the Heart of the Lakes Rydal Round, a fifteen-kilometre route around the Fairfield Horseshoe. I set off steadily, fairly near the front of the competitors, and felt OK. Five minutes into the first climb I started to feel really bad – tired, heavy legs and struggling to breathe – and loads of people started to overtake me. It was going to be a matter of surviving not racing. It was great to receive the encouragement of both my fellow runners, as they went past me, and the spectators, who understood why I was struggling so much. I managed to finish and even felt a little better for the last kilometre. I have no idea what time I did or where I finished, I was just happy to have finished.

Afterwards my legs felt tired but not sore, so two days later I decided to have a go at a much more serious challenge – the Borrowdale Fell Race. At twenty-seven kilometres long with 2,000 metres of ascent this takes in some of the Lake District's roughest terrain. My plan was again survival not racing. It was a wet day with the clouds down. Early on contouring round Glaramara I managed to go wrong and nearly ended up running back towards the start. The worst thing was I managed to lead about twenty other people following behind me the wrong way. After about ten minutes we were back on the route. I felt OK and was moving steadily until Great Gable but then I started to suffer. The climb to Dale Head was painful but the descent was probably even worse, I seemed to have lost all my coordination. I eventually finished in a time of four hours – my slowest by a long way. However, I was really happy to have finished and to be running in races again.

After Borrowdale I had a two-week family holiday in North Wales. I managed to do almost daily runs and eventually these went from being an effort to being enjoyable. On returning my timed run had reduced to seven minutes and thirteen seconds – still a bit off my best but another improvement. I then ran the Barrow Fell Race at Keswick Show where it was great to be racing again rather than just surviving.

Racing for the rest of the year was very up and down. I would do OK in a fell race, such as at the Three Shires Fell Race, or just feel completely shattered, as happened at the Langdale Horseshoe. The Lake District Mountain Trial (thirty-two kilometres long with 2,000 metres of ascent) was really hard work. I was exhausted on the last climb up to Great Dodd.

I slowed right down and eventually had to stop for a minute or so as I got really dizzy. Eventually I finished in over five hours in fourth place. The elite course at the OMM I did with Adam Perry and it was just hard work. I spent the whole weekend trying to keep up with Adam. This was despite giving him my rucksack, which weighed about four kilograms, for about half the time. Even worse was that although we were third fastest in a total time of twelve hours and eleven minutes, and only fourteen minutes behind the winners, we were declared non-competitive as we lost our electronic dibber which is used to record the times at the checkpoints. Although some of my race performances were reasonable, the worst thing was that it was taking ages to recover. For two weeks after the OMM I was absolutely shattered and unable to run, whereas normally within a week I am back to nearly full speed.

Around six months after my Wainwrights run I felt I had fully recovered. I started to train hard and gradually my results improved. After ten months I was getting close to my personal bests in races. But then my running speed instead of improving started to get worse. To start with the change was quite subtle – people who were normally behind me were beating me. As a runner you often have a little dip in form for no apparent reason and I thought it would pass. But the dip in form did not pass, it became worse. I took part in two fell races, the Duddon Fell Race and the Blencathra Fell Race, and in both did my worst-ever times despite trying really hard. All the way round I was struggling to breathe and had a tight chest. Normally after races I feel brilliant, but after these races I felt shivery. My resting heart rate was also about ten beats per minute higher than normal.

I thought I had just overdone the racing and training a bit so I took a couple of weeks completely off running and felt fine again. Then I started doing short and gentle runs at first and then slightly harder and longer runs, up to about an hour. I thought I was over whatever the problem was. I competed in the Sedbergh Hills Fell Race and took just over two and a half hours, which was about ten minutes longer than normal. I was happy with that, considering I had not done a large amount of training, and felt no ill effects afterwards. I also competed in the short Round Latrigg Race; again I was a bit slower than normal but happy that I felt fine afterwards. However, three days later I did an hour-long training run before breakfast and I was absolutely shattered while running and also after I had finished. I felt half asleep the whole time, a bit feverish, dizzy and unable to think clearly. I was definitely too tired to go out running for the next two weeks. This cycle then repeated itself. A rest, some gentle runs feeling good, then suddenly after a run feeling absolutely exhausted. Again I needed two weeks' recovery doing absolutely nothing. After this I went to the doctor and had a blood test but it found nothing unusual.

Since then I have been taking it easy and the symptoms have finally settled down and I can catalogue them, but thinking about it I now realise they have been around ever since I finished the Wainwrights run. I have just been ignoring them and trying to tell myself I feel fine. When I wake up in the morning after eight or nine hours' sleep, I do not feel refreshed in the slightest; in fact all I want to do is go back to bed. I ignore the urge to go back to bed but I still have this 'brain fog'. I cannot think straight or concentrate and my short-term memory is absolutely awful.

Emma: *'Steve has always been a bit hopeless, and his brain seems to take a long time to warm up in the morning, but since he finished the Wainwrights he's been worse than ever. Sometimes I will ask him a simple question like "what time are you finishing work today?", and it is as if I have spoken in a foreign language or asked for the answer to a complex mathematical equation. If he was a car he would probably need a new battery (and a few other parts) but unfortunately the human body is slightly more complicated. With hindsight he probably should have taken it easy for longer over the summer after he finished, but for someone who loves running so much that is easier said than done. He's coping with his current lack of running pretty well considering, I just hope that he gets back to his normal self sometime soon.'*

The brain fog normally clears around midday and by the evening I sometimes feel back to almost normal. On a good day it might clear at 10 a.m., on a bad day it might never clear. As well as this I am having a lot of headaches, quite a few disturbed nights, I quite often feel dizzy and I occasionally get fast and irregular heartbeats. Eventually I was referred for an ECG while I was having the strange heartbeats and this has been diagnosed as atrial fibrillation. Running hard, drinking alcohol and stress all make it worse, although I can happily do a short gentle jog and go walking without any problems. Lots of tests by the doctors have not found anything unusual, apart from the atrial fibrillation, and it seems once everything else has been ruled out they are left with the only other thing matching my symptoms – chronic fatigue syndrome (CFS). There is no medication available to specifically treat CFS, but a range of treatments to manage the physical and emotional effects.

So, I have mixed feelings about my recovery from the Wainwrights. I was prepared to push myself to the limit during those seven days in the knowledge that it would take a long time to recover, and also there was a real possibility of causing myself a long-term injury meaning it would be years before I could run again. So the fact that I do not have a long-term injury is good. But instead I have a more general problem, which is not just affecting my running but making me so tired and unable to concentrate that it is affecting the rest of my life including my work. It is now clear to me that the abuse I put my body through during the week of my Wainwrights has caught up with me. Afterwards I thought, 'I am not injured, I feel OK', and started running too hard too soon which in hindsight was a *big* mistake. But I enjoy running and racing so much it is hard for me not to leave the house and be out running on the fells.

As for the future, I feel confident the brain fog and other symptoms will soon go and at some point I will return to running at a top level. It might take months or maybe years but it will happen. The reason is that my mindset has finally changed. As a long-distance mountain runner I have always ignored my body when it tells me to stop. Over many years I have carried on pushing it and pushing it, accepting it hurts but ignoring the pain. Finally my body has had enough. So instead of fighting my body I now need to be very gentle and work with it. I can now happily accept that I am not going to run hard again until I have fully recovered and then wait a while afterwards. I am also going to avoid alcohol. Avoiding stresses in my life is harder but I know I can do it. I just need to relax and enjoy my work and it will become easier once I can think straight again. The human body has an amazing ability to recover if you look after it, and that is what I need to do.

EPILOGUE

There have been many changes since I completed the Wainwrights. Whenever I go to a fell race, orienteering event or mountain marathon I get loads of people congratulating me. For people to go out of their way to do this is really nice and I am always really touched. Then there is the film that Al Lee produced. I think Al did a brilliant job of capturing the whole week. There is the quiet start in Keswick with a few friends finding our way between the market stalls, then my gradual deterioration during the week and finally the amazing finish in Keswick with hundreds of people cheering me in. The Lake District fells are beautifully captured and it makes it obvious why I love running in them.

I have also been giving lots of talks about my Wainwrights run. To stand up in front of lots of people and talk is something I find very difficult. I get very nervous. But I do it for two reasons. Firstly, it is a great opportunity to raise more money for my MS charities. Any appearance money I receive from talks I always donate to the two charities. I raised over £20,000 for the two MS charities during the run. But this was money kindly donated by friends and family and people interested in my run. So I always thought the least I could do was donate any money I received from talking about my run to these charities. Secondly, many people are genuinely interested in my run. They want to find out everything they can about it – my preparations, how I coped with the blisters, how I recovered. The talks I do are a great way for people to find out about the week and ask me questions. The reaction I have had from my talks has always been positive and gradually I am becoming more relaxed doing them, and even beginning to enjoy them.

I am also happy to have won a variety of awards for my run. These include the Fell Runners Association Long Distance Award, UK Ultra Runners 'Hard as Nails' award, Ian Corless' Best International FKT (fastest known time) and I am now also one of *Cumbria Life* magazine's 'top 200 greatest Cumbrians'.

I hope you have enjoyed reading my account of the run. I have tried to write it from my heart and to tell the story both of my Wainwrights run and also my life story leading up to it, and in so doing, my motivations for running. I have found it difficult to put down on paper my emotions and what I went through while running the Wainwrights. Hopefully, together with the other contributors, I have managed to convey both the pain and the pleasure of running. I also hope I have managed to convey the amazing support I have received from my family and friends, without which I could never have been successful.

ACKNOWLEDGEMENTS

Huge thanks go to the many members of my support team who helped me on my Wainwrights run. These are acknowledged in the individual sections and I am extremely grateful for their help in enabling me to achieve my dream. Obviously Jane Saul was the key to organising all this help and I am extremely grateful for all the time and effort she put into sorting everything out. I would also like to thank other people not organised by Jane who turned up to either see me or run with me and also those who were present at the finish. Every single person was great, supportive and encouraging and contributed to an amazing week. I would also like to thank those people who generously helped look after my children during the week meaning that Emma could come out and see me at quite a lot of points. These include Joe and Mary Moody (Emma's parents), my mum, Tara Vallente, Mady Thompson and Sally Fielding.

I would like to thank Berghaus for their generous support of me as one of their athletes and their support of my Wainwrights run.

Of course, thanks go to my mum and dad for such a good job in bringing me up, and my siblings for putting up with me. I know I was a very difficult and stubborn child but over many years they always remained calm and positive, and my memory of my childhood is a happy one. My dad would have been so proud to have seen me run in and finish the Wainwrights at the Moot Hall in Keswick.

Without doubt a huge amount of my running success is down to Emma. I will always be very grateful for the support she gave me during my Wainwrights run and even more importantly her love, kindness and encouragement over many years. She has always supported my running and has been happy for me to go off and leave her for another weekend of training and racing. I know it was extremely hard for her to see me suffer so much over the week of the run and yet she always remained so strong. I would also like to thank my children for putting up with me being away from home training and racing, and also the cuddles they gave me at the support points on the run. I hope I have not put you off being in the fells and running.

Thanks to Tara Vallente for encouraging me to write this book and helping come up with the title. Also thanks to my sister, Karen, Heather Dawe and Liz Lewis for reading a draft copy of this book, suggesting improvements and encouraging me to get it published.

Finally, thanks to Vertebrate for the improvements they have made to the text and for publishing my book.

BIBLIOGRAPHY

Askwith, Richard, *Feet in the Clouds* (London: Aurum Press, 2004).

Chilton, Steve, *The Round: In Bob Graham's Footsteps* (Dingwall: Sandstone Press, 2015).

Naylor, Joss, *Joss Naylor MBE Was Here* (KLETS pamphlet, 1987).

Smith, Bill, *Stud Marks on the Summits* (Preston: SKG Publications, 1985).

Wainwright, Alfred, *The Complete Pictorial Guides: A Reader's Edition* (London: Frances Lincoln, 2008).

Wainwright, Alfred & Drabbs, Derry, *Fellwalking with Wainwright* (London: Michael Joseph, 1984).

APPENDIX
LIST OF WAINWRIGHT TIMINGS

Number	Wainwright Name	Date and Time		Split time
S1 (start)		14/06/2014	09:00	
1	Latrigg (368m)	14/06/2014	09:22	00:22
2	High Rigg (357m)	14/06/2014	10:04	00:42
3	Walla Crag (379m)	14/06/2014	10:42	00:38
4	Bleaberry Fell (590m)	14/06/2014	11:07	00:25
5	High Seat (608m)	14/06/2014	11:21	00:14
6	Raven Crag (461m)	14/06/2014	11:40	00:19
7	High Tove (515m)	14/06/2014	12:07	00:27
8	Armboth Fell (479m)	14/06/2014	12:15	00:08
9	Great Crag (450m)	14/06/2014	12:43	00:28
10	Grange Fell (415m)	14/06/2014	13:03	00:20
11	Castle Crag (298m)	14/06/2014	13:33	00:30
S1 (end)		14/06/2014	13:50	00:17
S2 (start)		14/06/2014	13:59	00:09
12	Rosthwaite Fell (551m)	14/06/2014	14:39	00:40
13	Glaramara (783m)	14/06/2014	15:18	00:39
14	Allen Crags (785m)	14/06/2014	15:46	00:28
15	Seathwaite Fell (601m)	14/06/2014	16:04	00:18
16	Base Brown (646m)	14/06/2014	16:34	00:30
17	Green Gable (801m)	14/06/2014	16:51	00:17
18	Great Gable (899m)	14/06/2014	17:06	00:15
19	Kirk Fell (802m)	14/06/2014	17:34	00:28
20	Brandreth (715m)	14/06/2014	18:02	00:28
21	Grey Knotts (697m)	14/06/2014	18:11	00:09
22	Fleetwith Pike (648m)	14/06/2014	18:36	00:25
23	Haystacks (597m)	14/06/2014	19:12	00:36
24	High Crag (744m)	14/06/2014	19:44	00:32
25	High Stile (806m)	14/06/2014	19:59	00:15
26	Red Pike, Buttermere (755m)	14/06/2014	20:13	00:14

27	Starling Dodd (633m)	14/06/2014	20:29	00:16
28	Great Bourne (616m)	14/06/2014	20:48	00:19
29	Hen Comb (509m)	14/06/2014	21:14	00:26
30	Mellbreak (512m)	14/06/2014	21:48	00:34
S2 (end)		14/06/2014	22:17	00:29
S3 (start)		14/06/2014	22:37	00:20
31	Low Fell (423m)	14/06/2014	23:12	00:35
32	Fellbarrow (416m)	14/06/2014	23:32	00:20
33	Burnbank Fell (475m)	15/06/2014	00:33	01:01
34	Blake Fell (573m)	15/06/2014	00:48	00:15
35	Gavel Fell (526m)	15/06/2014	01:04	00:16
S3 (end)		15/06/2014	01:49	00:45
S4 (start)		15/06/2014	05:04	03:15
36	Grike (488m)	15/06/2014	05:38	00:34
37	Crag Fell (523m)	15/06/2014	05:51	00:13
38	Lank Rigg (541m)	15/06/2014	06:26	00:35
39	Caw Fell (697m)	15/06/2014	07:25	00:59
40	Haycock (797m)	15/06/2014	07:43	00:18
41	Steeple (819m)	15/06/2014	08:04	00:21
42	Scoat Fell (841m)	15/06/2014	08:11	00:07
43	Pillar (892m)	15/06/2014	08:36	00:25
44	Red Pike, Wasdale (826m)	15/06/2014	09:03	00:27
45	Yewbarrow (628m)	15/06/2014	09:40	00:37
46	Seatallan (692m)	15/06/2014	10:59	01:19
47	Middle Fell (582m)	15/06/2014	11:22	00:23
48	Buckbarrow (423m)	15/06/2014	11:49	00:27
S4 (end)		15/06/2014	12:16	00:27
S5 (start)		15/06/2014	12:36	00:20
49	Whin Rigg (535m)	15/06/2014	13:23	00:47
50	Illgill Head (609m)	15/06/2014	13:51	00:28
51	Slight Side (762m)	15/06/2014	14:59	01:08
52	Scafell (964m)	15/06/2014	15:26	00:27
53	Lingmell (807m)	15/06/2014	16:14	00:48
54	Scafell Pike (978m)	15/06/2014	16:45	00:31
55	Great End (910m)	15/06/2014	17:13	00:28
56	Esk Pike (885m)	15/06/2014	17:38	00:25
57	Rossett Pike (651m)	15/06/2014	18:02	00:24
58	Bow Fell (902m)	15/06/2014	18:34	00:32

59	Crinkle Crags (859m)	15/06/2014	19:10	00:36
60	Pike o' Blisco (705m)	15/06/2014	19:50	00:40
61	Cold Pike (701m)	15/06/2014	20:17	00:27
62	Hard Knott (549m)	15/06/2014	21:16	00:59
S5 (end)		15/06/2014	21:25	00:09
S6 (start)		15/06/2014	21:35	00:10
63	Harter Fell, Eskdale (654m)	15/06/2014	22:08	00:33
64	Green Crag (489m)	15/06/2014	22:46	00:38
S6 (end)		15/06/2014	23:28	00:42
S7 (start)		16/06/2014	04:36	05:08
65	Dow Crag (778m)	16/06/2014	05:40	01:04
66	Coniston Old Man (803m)	16/06/2014	06:02	00:22
67	Brim Fell (796m)	16/06/2014	06:12	00:10
68	Grey Friar (773m)	16/06/2014	06:41	00:29
69	Great Carrs (785m)	16/06/2014	06:56	00:15
70	Swirl How (802m)	16/06/2014	07:01	00:05
71	Wetherlam (762m)	16/06/2014	07:33	00:32
S7 (end)		16/06/2014	08:08	00:35
S8 (start)		16/06/2014	08:25	00:17
72	Holme Fell (317m)	16/06/2014	08:45	00:20
73	Black Fell (322m)	16/06/2014	09:39	00:54
74	Lingmoor Fell (469m)	16/06/2014	10:52	01:13
S8 (end)		16/06/2014	11:15	00:23
S9 (start)		16/06/2014	11:45	00:30
75	Loft Crag (680m)	16/06/2014	12:34	00:49
76	Pike of Stickle (709m)	16/06/2014	12:43	00:09
77	Harrison Stickle (736m)	16/06/2014	12:57	00:14
78	Pavey Ark (700m)	16/06/2014	13:07	00:10
79	Thunacar Knott (723m)	16/06/2014	13:15	00:08
80	Sergeant Man (736m)	16/06/2014	13:30	00:15
81	High Raise, Langdale (762m)	16/06/2014	13:39	00:09
82	Sergeant's Crag (571m)	16/06/2014	13:57	00:18
83	Eagle Crag (525m)	16/06/2014	14:06	00:09
84	Ullscarf (726m)	16/06/2014	14:51	00:45
85	Steel Fell (553m)	16/06/2014	15:31	00:40
86	Calf Crag (537m)	16/06/2014	16:08	00:37
87	Gibson Knott (420m)	16/06/2014	16:33	00:25
88	Helm Crag (405m)	16/06/2014	16:45	00:12
89	Tarn Crag (550m)	16/06/2014	17:37	00:52

90	Blea Rigg (541m)	16/06/2014	18:11	00:34
91	Silver How (395m)	16/06/2014	18:41	00:30
92	Loughrigg Fell (335m)	16/06/2014	19:24	00:43
S9 (end)		16/06/2014	19:46	00:22
S10 (start)		17/06/2014	01:10	05:24
93	Nab Scar (450m)	17/06/2014	01:42	00:32
94	Heron Pike (612m)	17/06/2014	02:00	00:18
95	Stone Arthur (500m)	17/06/2014	02:25	00:25
96	Great Rigg (766m)	17/06/2014	02:50	00:25
97	Seat Sandal (736m)	17/06/2014	03:27	00:37
98	Fairfield (873m)	17/06/2014	04:00	00:33
99	Hart Crag (822m)	17/06/2014	04:16	00:16
100	Hartsop above How (570m)	17/06/2014	04:38	00:22
101	Dove Crag (792m)	17/06/2014	05:08	00:30
102	High Pike, Scandale (656m)	17/06/2014	05:21	00:13
103	Low Pike (508m)	17/06/2014	05:45	00:24
104	Little Hart Crag (637m)	17/06/2014	06:33	00:48
105	High Hartsop Dodd (519m)	17/06/2014	06:40	00:07
106	Middle Dodd (654m)	17/06/2014	07:15	00:35
107	Red Screes (776m)	17/06/2014	07:29	00:14
S10 (end)		17/06/2014	07:41	00:12
S11 (start)		17/06/2014	08:40	00:59
108	Stony Cove Pike (763m)	17/06/2014	09:22	00:42
109	Hartsop Dodd (618m)	17/06/2014	09:38	00:16
110	Gray Crag (698m)	17/06/2014	10:31	00:53
111	Thornthwaite Crag (784m)	17/06/2014	10:53	00:22
112	Froswick (720m)	17/06/2014	11:09	00:16
113	Ill Bell (757m)	17/06/2014	11:23	00:14
114	Yoke (706m)	17/06/2014	11:34	00:11
115	Troutbeck Tongue (364m)	17/06/2014	12:13	00:39
116	Wansfell (487m)	17/06/2014	12:59	00:46
S11 (end)		17/06/2014	13:22	00:23
S12 (start)		17/06/2014	13:58	00:36
117	Sour Howes (483m)	17/06/2014	14:32	00:34
118	Sallows (516m)	17/06/2014	14:47	00:15
S12 (end)		17/06/2014	15:27	00:40
S13 (start)		17/06/2014	16:25	00:58
119	Shipman Knotts (587m)	17/06/2014	17:01	00:36
120	Kentmere Pike (730m)	17/06/2014	17:21	00:20
121	Tarn Crag (664m)	17/06/2014	18:00	00:39

122	Grey Crag (638m)	17/06/2014	18:15	00:15
123	Selside Pike (655m)	17/06/2014	19:13	00:58
124	Branstree (713m)	17/06/2014	19:34	00:21
125	Harter Fell, Mardale (778m)	17/06/2014	20:13	00:39
126	Mardale Ill Bell (760m)	17/06/2014	20:51	00:38
127	High Street (828m)	17/06/2014	21:03	00:12
128	The Knott (739m)	17/06/2014	21:22	00:19
129	Rampsgill Head (792m)	17/06/2014	21:32	00:10
130	Kidsty Pike (780m)	17/06/2014	21:37	00:05
131	High Raise, High Street (802m)	17/06/2014	21:50	00:13
132	Wether Hill (670m)	17/06/2014	22:16	00:26
133	Loadpot Hill (671m)	17/06/2014	22:33	00:17
134	Arthur's Pike (533m)	17/06/2014	23:00	00:27
135	Bonscale Pike (524m)	17/06/2014	23:16	00:16
S13 (end)		17/06/2014	23:57	00:41
S14 (start)		18/06/2014	05:13	05:16
136	Hallin Fell (388m)	18/06/2014	05:30	00:17
137	Steel Knotts (432m)	18/06/2014	06:13	00:43
138	Beda Fell (509m)	18/06/2014	06:59	00:46
139	The Nab (576m)	18/06/2014	07:54	00:55
140	Rest Dodd (696m)	18/06/2014	08:17	00:23
141	Brock Crags (561m)	18/06/2014	08:34	00:17
142	Angletarn Pikes (567m)	18/06/2014	08:51	00:17
143	Place Fell (657m)	18/06/2014	09:28	00:37
S14 (end)		18/06/2014	09:59	00:31
S15 (start)		18/06/2014	10:59	01:00
144	Arnison Crag (433m)	18/06/2014	11:23	00:24
145	Birks (622m)	18/06/2014	11:52	00:29
146	St Sunday Crag (841m)	18/06/2014	12:22	00:30
147	Dollywaggon Pike (858m)	18/06/2014	13:21	00:59
148	Nethermost Pike (891m)	18/06/2014	13:40	00:19
149	Helvellyn (950m)	18/06/2014	13:55	00:15
150	Catstye Cam (890m)	18/06/2014	14:14	00:19
151	Birkhouse Moor (718m)	18/06/2014	14:37	00:23
S15 (end)		18/06/2014	15:12	00:35
S16 (start)		18/06/2014	16:02	00:50
152	Glenridding Dodd (442m)	18/06/2014	16:26	00:24
153	Sheffield Pike (675m)	18/06/2014	17:00	00:34
154	Hart Side (756m)	18/06/2014	17:33	00:33
155	Raise (883m)	18/06/2014	18:14	00:41

156	White Side (863m)	18/06/2014	18:22	00:08
157	Stybarrow Dodd (843m)	18/06/2014	18:52	00:30
158	Watson's Dodd (789m)	18/06/2014	19:02	00:10
159	Great Dodd (857m)	18/06/2014	19:16	00:14
160	Clough Head (726m)	18/06/2014	19:47	00:31
S16 (end)		18/06/2014	21:00	01:13
S17 (start)		18/06/2014	21:53	00:53
161	Gowbarrow Fell (481m)	18/06/2014	22:17	00:24
162	Little Mell Fell (505m)	18/06/2014	23:00	00:43
163	Great Mell Fell (537m)	18/06/2014	23:53	00:53
S17 (end)		19/06/2014	00:25	00:32
S18 (start)		19/06/2014	05:53	05:28
164	Souther Fell (522m)	19/06/2014	06:52	00:59
165	Blencathra (868m)	19/06/2014	07:43	00:51
166	Mungrisdale Common (633m)	19/06/2014	08:07	00:24
167	Bannerdale Crags (683m)	19/06/2014	08:36	00:29
168	Bowscale Fell (702m)	19/06/2014	08:57	00:21
S18 (end)		19/06/2014	09:23	00:26
S19 (start)		19/06/2014	10:02	00:39
169	Carrock Fell (661m)	19/06/2014	10:44	00:42
170	High Pike, Caldbeck (658m)	19/06/2014	11:18	00:34
171	Knott (710m)	19/06/2014	11:58	00:40
172	Great Sca Fell (651m)	19/06/2014	12:07	00:09
173	Brae Fell (586m)	19/06/2014	12:21	00:14
174	Longlands Fell (483m)	19/06/2014	12:45	00:24
175	Meal Fell (550m)	19/06/2014	13:18	00:33
176	Great Cockup (526m)	19/06/2014	13:40	00:22
177	Great Calva (690m)	19/06/2014	14:40	01:00
S19 (end)		19/06/2014	15:18	00:38
S19a (start)		19/06/2014	15:46	00:28
178	Bakestall (673m)	19/06/2014	16:05	00:19
179	Skiddaw (931m)	19/06/2014	16:36	00:31
180	Lonscale Fell (715m)	19/06/2014	17:16	00:40
181	Little Man (865m)	19/06/2014	17:45	00:29
182	Carl Side (746m)	19/06/2014	18:08	00:23
183	Long Side (734m)	19/06/2014	18:15	00:07
184	Ullock Pike (690m)	19/06/2014	18:25	00:10
185	Dodd (502m)	19/06/2014	19:10	00:45
S19a (end)		19/06/2014	19:35	00:25

S20 (start)		19/06/2014	20:43	01:08
186	Binsey (447m)	19/06/2014	22:14	01:31
S20 (end)		19/06/2014	23:25	01:11
S21 (start)		20/06/2014	05:30	06:05
187	Sale Fell (359m)	20/06/2014	05:51	00.21
188	Ling Fell (373m)	20/06/2014	06:19	00:28
189	Graystones (452m)	20/06/2014	06:54	00:35
190	Broom Fell (511m)	20/06/2014	07:22	00:28
191	Lord's Seat (552m)	20/06/2014	07:34	00:12
192	Barf (468m)	20/06/2014	07:44	00:10
193	Whinlatter (517m)	20/06/2014	08:34	00:50
S21 (end)		20/06/2014	08:58	00:24
S22 (start)		20/06/2014	09:53	00:55
194	Grisedale Pike (791m)	20/06/2014	10:44	00:51
195	Hopegill Head (770m)	20/06/2014	11:10	00:26
196	Whiteside (707m)	20/06/2014	11:26	00:16
S22 (end)		20/06/2014	12:10	00:44
S23 (start)		20/06/2014	13:05	00:55
197	Rannerdale Knotts (355m)	20/06/2014	13:30	00:25
198	Whiteless Pike (660m)	20/06/2014	14:12	00:42
199	Wandope (772m)	20/06/2014	14:34	00:22
200	Grasmoor (852m)	20/06/2014	14:57	00:23
201	Crag Hill (839m)	20/06/2014	15:30	00:33
202	Sail (773m)	20/06/2014	15:38	00:08
203	Scar Crags (672m)	20/06/2014	15:51	00:13
204	Causey Pike (637m)	20/06/2014	16:03	00:12
205	Barrow (455m)	20/06/2014	16:36	00:33
206	Outerside (568m)	20/06/2014	17:01	00:25
207	Ard Crags (581m)	20/06/2014	17:36	00:35
208	Knott Rigg (556m)	20/06/2014	17:51	00:15
S23 (end)		20/06/2014	18:03	00:12
S24 (start)		20/06/2014	18:21	00:18
209	Robinson (737m)	20/06/2014	19:00	00:39
210	Hindscarth (727m)	20/06/2014	19:25	00:25
211	Dale Head (753m)	20/06/2014	19:45	00:20
212	High Spy (653m)	20/06/2014	20:19	00:34
213	Maiden Moor (576m)	20/06/2014	20:40	00:21
214	Cat Bells (451m)	20/06/2014	21:04	00:24
S24 (end)		20/06/2014	22:01	00:57